GRACE

activated

*Unlocking and unleashing the
limitless gift of grace*

SAM ADEYEMI

Acknowledgments

It took a collection of amazing people across continents to bring this book to reality. I wish to express my appreciation to them here.

Toye Sobande, Ezekiel Akinrinade, and Oluwatoyin Olanrewaju worked hard on the first draft of the manuscript. I appreciate Rotimi Kehinde and the staff at Kingdom Branding for the structure and editing, and for following through on the publishing of the US edition. I appreciate the hardworking staff at Daystar Christian Centre that combed through the archives to source content, and the staff at Pneuma Publishing Limited for working hard to get the edition published in Nigeria out under tight deadlines.

Let me appreciate Olatunbosun Sowunmi, a pastor and a protégé based in Calgary Canada, for inspiring the idea and ordering hundreds of copies even before the book was published. Talk about being motivated! I appreciate my family, friends, mentors, and colleagues in our organizations, which have offered encouragement along the way.

I sincerely appreciate my sweetheart, Adenike, who has been my partner in experiencing God's grace. We have enjoyed God's grace in amazing ways. I appreciate our children, Sophie, David, and Adora, for their understanding and support. Finally, I thank you, the reader, for getting your copy of this book. That is what makes writing and publishing it worth the while.

Contents

Contents

1

The Power of Grace

"But by the grace of God, I am what I am..."

For over a decade now, the church has placed a strong emphasis on faith. That emphasis is not misplaced by any account because the Bible states clearly that the just shall live by faith.[1] However, the Bible also says, "For by grace you have been saved through faith, and that not of yourselves; it is the gift of God, not of works, lest anyone should boast."[2] This presents a road map to understanding the relationship between faith and grace. You'll notice that faith, here, is only a means to an end.

---

1 Romans 1:17
2 Ephesians 2:8

The power that gets the job done is grace; however, faith is the means. Likewise, you cannot get grace to be active without the presence of faith. Both are important concepts, and both work hand in hand, but the real issue and the subject of our focus is grace. This is because this verse is referring to the most important event that could ever happen in the life of a human being: the free gift of salvation.

The root cause of human misery and problems is sin. Many go through their lives, not understanding how to correctly analyze their problems because the number one problem every human being has is the sin problem. Despite the many challenges we face, we have been able to invent so many things to meet our needs, but the sin problem has remained and still remains the one problem that no man has been able to solve. No man has been able to present the fix to the sin condition except Jesus, who was fully God and fully man. His solution is simple for us: *For you know the grace of our Lord Jesus Christ, that though He was rich, yet for your sake, He became poor, that you through His poverty may become rich.*

In the church, we talk a whole lot about healing, prosperity, divine favor, divine promotion, but I tell you, these are only fringe benefits attached to salvation. Before sin came into our world, there was no poverty, theft, murder, sickness, or premature death. Sin brought all of those ills in its contract. We try to treat the symptoms without understanding the deeper underlying cause.

When God wants to deal with all the negatives in your life, the first thing He does is deal with the sin. At the root is sin, and all those ills are the fruits of sin. There is no point in God taking away the fruit without removing the root because the fruits will only come back if the root is not dealt with.

In this book, I am writing about the power that solves the root problem. It is grace. Grace solves the root problem. And if grace is strong enough to deal with sin, you can rest assured that grace can deal with everything else. If it is by grace that you are saved, then it is by grace that you are healed. It is by grace that you become prosperous. It is by grace that you fulfill your marital destiny. It is by grace that you get a job! Amen!

Let's revisit that scripture and dig a little deeper: *For by grace, you have been saved **through faith.** It says, even that thing is not of yourself, **it is a gift from God.*** So, when you understand the true definition of grace, you realize that even faith is a product of grace because grace actually means gift – undeserved gift. To experience the grace of God is to receive something that you do not deserve or that you are not qualified to get.

We have all sinned and come short of the glory of God.[3] We will never qualify for forgiveness of sins, no matter what we do. There is absolutely nothing we can ever do, humanly speaking, that will qualify us for the mercy of God. Even in the Old Testament, the blood of sheep and goats was a temporary covering for sin and never fixed the sin condition. But the grace of God is freely given to us through His son, Jesus. For the wages of sin is death, but the free gift of God is eternal life through Jesus Christ.[4]

Salvation is a gift. Righteousness is a gift. However, receiving these gifts seems to be the big issue for many Christians. You have to learn how to receive. Salvation is not of works and does not require human effort to actualize. Your works will never qualify you for the blessings of God. Period.

3 Romans 3:23
4 Romans 6:23

I know personally that our teachings on faith impress on us to believe and confess. Some people have confessed so many times that they are now confused because it is not the confession that actually moves God. Confessing is your own part, but God still has to do His own part for the equation to be complete. He has a right to do it or not to do it.

You see, what I have discovered is that we exercise so much faith that we now have more faith in our faith than in the grace of God. Let that sink in for a moment.

We put so much emphasis on our faith that we begin to think we must receive those things that we ask for based on what we have done. Sorry, that is not how it works. The Apostle Paul declared that "I have planted, Apollos has watered, but it is God that gives the increase."[5] If God does not bring the increase, there is absolutely nothing your works can do to make it happen. That's why you need to "re-understand" the power of grace.

Grace is a gift

Let me paint a picture of what it is like for a Christian who has not learned how to live by grace. Apostle Paul said, "By the grace of God, I am what I am."[6] Outside of the grace of God, you cannot become the person that God wants you to be. It is by the grace of God that you have a new identity in Christ. A person outside of grace will toil, and that, in fact, is a curse.

Any attempt to secure God's blessings through human effort will result in frustration. James made that very clear when

5 1st Corinthians 3:6
6 1 Corinthians 15:10

he wrote, *"Where do wars and fights come from among you? Do they not come from your desires for pleasure that war in your members? You lust and do not have. You murder and covet and cannot obtain. You fight and war, yet you do not have because you do not ask. You ask and do not receive because you ask amiss, that you may spend it on your pleasures. Adulterers and adulteresses! Do you not know that friendship with the world is enmity with God? Whoever therefore wants to be a friend of the world makes himself an enemy of God."* [7]

Do you know that he wrote this to Christians? He said, "You war, you covet, you try to get, you cannot obtain." Why? He said, "In the first place, you don't even ask, you just try to get."

When a person has not learned to rely on God or to trust God completely, that person's life will be very shallow. You'll have a person looking for escape routes and quick fixes. There are way too many people in churches looking for formulas and magical solutions. You'll hear them saying things like, "What did they say we should do?"

Remember, it's not about what you do. **What you seek is a gift, and as long as you want to pay for it, God will not allow you to get it.** God determines the terms by which you get it. You cannot pay for something that God has already labeled a gift. How can you pay for a package that is clearly labeled "GIFT"? How does that work? Can you imagine deciding to give someone a car, and then the person asks you, "How much is it? How much can I pay you for it?" or "I'm going to work so hard so I can afford to pay you for the car you have offered as a gift." It simply doesn't make sense.

---

7 James 4:1-4 (NKJV)

As long as you, a Christian, are trying to pay for what God has labeled a gift, He will not allow you to get it until you get to the end of yourself when all your attempts to pay have been frustrated. You might even think the reason for the delay or the problem is a demon, but it is not. Listen, it is in your destiny to have a beautiful family, but as long as you are trying to control everything and everyone and get that "amazing family" by works, it will only end in frustration. Having a successful family is a gift. You can do everything that you are supposed to as a parent or spouse and still end up with family issues.

You might be the most beautiful lady, have a degree, a fantastic job, and still not have a husband or a good one at that. That is life. You can have a first-class degree and not be able to find a job or keep one. The fact is that you need the grace of God to succeed.

In the business sector, you need the grace of God to get a contract. You need the grace of God to live in good health. On the streets of our urban cities, you need the grace of God not to have someone run into your brand-new car. On a lighter note, I remember many years ago when I was learning how to drive. I was told to assume that every other driver on the road was crazy so I could be on my guard and respond if anything were to happen suddenly. I would breathe a sigh of relief after making it through the roads of Lagos, Nigeria, without a scratch. Safe driving even takes the grace of God!

The Enemies of Grace

Pride

Do you know that the Bible says "God resists the proud

and gives grace to the humble?"[8] Let me repeat it. Anyone who tries to qualify for God's blessings through his/her own efforts will have God standing in their way, not some demon. God resists the proud. I have seen very brilliant people fail examinations because they thought it was all about their intelligence. I have seen people who were qualified with all types of qualifications, and yet, things still did not work out for them. In fact, I was one of them.

Being highly connected is no guarantee, especially when you are born again. I remember trying to use one of my "connections" on a particular issue. One day, the Holy Spirit told me clearly: "Stop embarrassing these "powerful" people. Stop embarrassing them. You are asking them to help you, and because they have reverence for you, they try to help, but they fail. They successfully help others but fail when it comes to you. Leave them alone! It is not the devil. I am the one that is not allowing their efforts to work out. If I don't help you, nobody can help you."

By the grace of God, I am what I am. God resists or frustrates the proud and gives grace to the humble. Here's the good news. You and I can never have enough qualifications for salvation, but you know what happened? We got saved despite our lack of qualifications. We made it into God's family! Isn't that good news? Why? Because salvation is a gift. All we did, on our own part, was listen to God's word, believe, then we got saved. God did it!

Lack of Identity

If we could receive salvation, we can also get everything else. Not by human effort, but by the grace of God. The basis

---

8 James 4:6

of grace is the finished work of Jesus Christ on the cross of Calvary; this is the only qualification we have. You need to understand who you are and what Christ has done. The lack of understanding of our identity in Christ is a showstopper. "For He has made Him to be sin for us who knew no sin, that we may be made the righteousness of God in Christ."[9]

You see that? We were sinners, but He was sinless. On the cross of Calvary, He became sin personified so that we could become sinless. So today, in the eyes of God, because of the grace of God, we are sinless. Once you believe this, just accept it through faith. You accept that Jesus took your sins on the cross of Calvary. You are no longer a sinner, and you are righteous. That's how it works. It's really that simple. You've been struggling against sin and trying to overpower that sinful habit; you've read all the books on how to break habits, but still, nothing works. Here's the secret.

Works & Self-Determination

Determination is not enough. Do you know how many have determined that they would not commit adultery? You can have tons of mp3s on holiness and still commit sin. You don't know how strong sin is. Sin is not just an idea; it is not just a psychological influence. It is a spiritual reality. All you have to do is accept that there is therefore now no condemnation to them who are in Christ Jesus, who walk not after the flesh, but after the Spirit. The law of the Spirit of Life in Christ Jesus has made you free from the law of sin and death.[10] When temptation comes, pray with this reality and ask the Holy Spirit to help you. You will be amazed by how the issue will be resolved, especially if you are fully committed to doing whatever the Holy Spirit tells you to do.

---

9 2nd Corinthians 5:21
10 Romans 8:1

What about healing? By His stripes, you were healed.[11] The same cross. What about prosperity? The Bible says, "For you know the grace of our Lord Jesus Christ, that though He was rich, yet for your sakes He became poor, that you through His poverty may become rich."[12] Just believe what Christ has already done, then do whatever He tells you to do. That is all!

Are you struggling to breakthrough? That's the recipe for a breakdown. You need grace. It is done by grace. I have tasted poverty, and now I am blessed financially. I know the difference.

If I had gone by what I tried to work out for myself, I would not be anywhere near where I am today. I have experienced the type of grace that when some things happen, I would lay down prostrate and say "thank you" to God because I knew there was no other way I could have gotten those breakthroughs.

People I have read about in newspapers in the past are now my friends. The people I watched on television are now my friends. That can only be grace! Promotion does not come from the east or the west or south. It comes from God, who is the judge of all. He lifts up one person and puts down another one.

I pray for you as you read this book, that miracles of grace will happen in your life in the name of Jesus Christ. You have declared for too long. You have confessed too many times, but without the grace of God, all of that can result in nothing. You must make room for the sovereignty of God.

---

11 1 Peter 2:24
12 2nd Corinthians 8:9

Keep abiding by the principles of God. Continue to give sacrificially and to work hard, but the power of grace is the guarantee for a breakthrough.

Do not brag about what you have been doing. It is time to put your faith in what God can do. Satisfying the principles is like doing all the electrical work in a new building and putting all the fittings in place, but if there is no power supply, all that work will be useless. You can't see electricity with your natural eyes, and that is precisely how the grace of God is. It is this invisible force that rests upon your life and powers your life. All of a sudden, the things that weren't working before in your life begin to work.

Discovering the Power in Grace

Everything you need to live a successful life is already around you. The relationships you need are around you. All the money you need is around you, but it is the grace of God that will make them come alive for you. If you are looking for a job, I pray for you that you will get an even better one. If you can't afford to buy your own home by human calculation, through grace, you will buy it. There is a God that rules in the affairs of men. He appoints kings and removes kings. If someone or something is in your way, they will be moved from your path through the grace of God.

You may have been searching for the missing piece. I can assure you that you're about to experience a life-changing phenomenon. Grace is so potent that when it is upon a life, it is simply unstoppable. It has lifted up the weak and empowered the broken. It has been in effect in the greatest tragedies and in the most astonishing triumphs. Grace brought the creator of the universe through His love for humanity to a horrible death on the cross. It was in full effect on the cross.

The grace of God is so strong and powerful. God can remove presidents for the sake of a believer. There will be a miracle of grace in your life as you read this book. Whatever it is that you have lost is being restored back to you. I prophesy by the grace of God that you will not die, you will live, and your destiny will find fulfillment in the name of Jesus Christ.

2

Candidate for Grace

"For when I am weak, then I am strong."

When God brings about dramatic changes in your life, it will be unmistakable. You will know it is God that did it, and that is why it will usually not happen in any normal circumstance. When God steps in, the signs will be evident, and all will know that is it not by human wisdom or power, it is only by the grace of God. In this chapter, we'll discuss who a candidate for grace is.

Paul said, "But he said to me, "My grace is sufficient for you, for my power is made perfect in weakness." Therefore I will boast all the more gladly about my weaknesses, so that Christ's power may rest on me."[1]

---

1 2 Corinthians 12: 9

Paul was a candidate for grace because he had to deal with unfavorable circumstances. Anyone who has had to face challenges or a difficult situation is a candidate for grace. Take, for instance, a husband or wife dealing with a spouse that is not saved; or dealing with someone irresponsible or juvenile. How do you deal with pain? How do you handle crises? How do you deal with difficulties? I'm talking about issues that are pressing like a wayward child, financial crises, or a life-threatening health condition. How do you deal with an academic situation that seems like a guaranteed failure?

That fact that Apostle Paul said, "And lest I should be exalted above measure by the abundance of the revelation, a thorn in the flesh was given to me," – is remarkable. Don't forget that Paul was an anointed man. He was someone who had things going on well for him. His ministry was growing, and he had no shortage of crowds. There were miracles and signs at work in his life. But, with all that success, there was also a source of pain in his life.

So, when you see a visibly blessed person, don't ever assume that their lives are perfect. There's something about the way we put people on pedestals that makes us disappointed when we discover a point of weakness in their lives. No one

has it all to perfection. With all the glam and notoriety, with all the fame and money, there is always a "but." But maybe there is a purpose to the "but." Let's dig deeper.

The Relationship between Pain and Grace

As a student of grace, don't quickly react to the things you see on the outside, because if you have spiritual eyes, you will soon discover that the handicap or weakness is one of the reasons the person is blessed. If only you had the spiritual

eyes to see. We have been conditioned to believe that the best outcome of any pain or challenge we experience is for us to receive relief from whatever is causing the pain. We have come to believe that the perfect life, the best life is one without pain or handicap whatsoever.

As soon as we are faced with pain, the first thing we want to do is to get rid of it. We believe that the proof of God in our lives is not to have any pain whatsoever.

Apostle Paul felt the same way. He began to pray, and I paraphrase, "Lord, take it out. I can't be this anointed and have this issue. Take it out, Lord! How can I be this anointed and successful in ministry and still have to deal with this?" What God eventually showed him is that there was indeed a connection between His pain and His grace. There was a connection between that pain and the anointing on his life. That anointing was going to be cut short if God did not keep him in touch with his humanity.

There is something so vain about the human mind that is it is quite difficult for us to separate our sense of worth from our achievements and accomplishments. The more we achieve or attain success, the more inflated our egos, and the more we are deceived into thinking we are what we are not. It is important to avoid this deceptive trap. The Apostle Paul had to ask, "What have you that you have not received? If you have received it, why are you behaving as if you did not receive it?"[2] John the Baptist also declared, "A man can receive nothing except it is given him from above."[3] This powerful truth is sadly often lost in our way of thinking, especially when everything seems to be working well for us.

---

2 1 Corinthians 4:7
3 John 3:27

Moses had to warn Israel, "You see the Land that God is taking you to, it is good land. You will prosper there beyond your imagination, possess houses you did not build, you will eat bread without scarcity."[4] In other words, he was saying, "Listen, things are going to work for you. Yes! You will live in good houses and have livestock in abundance; you will have money and resources, but beware, lest after things have worked for you, you start believing it was all by your own power."

Think about what happened to Herod. Only God knows how many times he had performed his song before his day of reckoning. Can you picture him singing off-key? That is the problem when you have a king or leader with sycophants around him or her. This is a big part of the problem that comes with success. When things are working for you, some people derive their sense of relevance just from being around you, and they are the ones who confuse you and inflate your ego with their praises.

Herod took the stage singing, and the people began to applaud voraciously, hailing his voice as the voice of a god and not of a man. There he was nodding his head and accepting their praise. The voice of a god? He had forgotten who gave him his voice in the first place. The next moment, an angel struck him, and worms began to eat his body right where he was standing, and he fell down dead.

The Evidence of Grace

Let's get back into our deep dive into Apostle Paul's life. The kind of anointing that was on him was heavy. There was a kind of anointing reserved for the twelve disciples who walked with Jesus. It was a unique grace that was

4 Deuteronomy 8:9

reserved for them. For instance, Apostle Paul had once been a notorious sinner, a Pharisee who was far from being born again when the disciples were walking with Jesus. It was, in fact, after Jesus had resurrected and gone to heaven that Paul went crazy, arresting Christians and throwing them into prison. He was the one who supervised the death of Stephen, allowing the mob to place their clothes at his feet as they stoned Stephen.

In spite of that track record, this was still the man God met with on the way to Damascus. In a dramatic fashion, he saw Jesus and heard His voice. Regardless of his past, he could now make the same claim as the other "powerful" disciples that he had seen and heard the Lord. So, as you can see, the grace on his life was heavy, really heavy. Paul said, and I paraphrase, "When they (those powerful disciples) perceived the grace of God that was on Barnabas and myself, they gave us the right hand of fellowship. They could not keep us out because it was evident that what we were doing was pure grace from God."[5]

There was even a time when the Apostle Paul wrote in a letter to the church in Corinth. He was "caught up" to the third heavens, where he received so many revelations.

There were some which he was not permitted to share with humans. That is how graced this former tormentor of the church was.

Think about it! Can you imagine being so close to God that you learn about secrets that you cannot share with other human beings, and yet have a handicap? Of course, Paul's first reaction, like anyone of us, was to cry out to God for deliverance, but afterward, he came to understand the true purpose of that handicap. He said, as quoted from The

5 Galatians 2:9

Message translation, that "Because of the extravagance of those revelations and so I wouldn't get a big head, I was given the gift of a handicap to keep me in constant touch with my limitations."[6]

Imperfect Perfection

Sometimes, we think we know ourselves until promotion comes. Then, our craziness is unleashed. We are capable of doing crazy things when we have the means. Study the Word, and you will discover stories of people that God promoted, who went from kind and loving to just crazy. But Apostle Paul came to realize that what the enemy thought would get him down was, in fact, what pushed him to his knees before God. That's the key! It is a total dependence on God.

When you have a handicap, regardless of your successes, you come to realize that you won't be able to walk around all high and mighty like you achieved anything in your own strength. Even when people praise you, remember that you are no god. While everyone is assuming your life is perfect and liking your social media posts, remember you are not. We're all facing different handicaps at different levels.

At first, Paul didn't realize his handicap was a blessing in disguise. He begged God to remove it three times, and then God told him, "My grace is enough. My strength comes into its own in your weakness."[7] So, whatever it is that has not been working in your life, you have a choice. You can focus on the pain, or you can focus on grace. Most people make the mistake of focusing on the pain. Focusing on the pain brings bitterness. But, if you focus on grace, you will not end up bitter, but better. **The handicap is not a cap on**

6 2 Corinthians 12:9
7 2 Corinthians 12:9

your life.

Pain and Pearls

I remember learning about how the oyster in the ocean develops pearls, and it completely changed my perspective of pain. When a grain of sand enters an oyster's shell, it gets irritated and begins to do everything possible to get the grain of sand out. When this is unsuccessful, the oyster then secretes a fluid, which solidifies around the grain of sand, and soon, it will not feel the prickling irritation from the grain of sand anymore. Guess what? Eventually, the fluid becomes a pearl, which is tremendously valuable to human beings.

You can also secrete something of value when you go through pain. What God squeezes out of you is the anointing; it is grace, and it is of tremendous value. That is the thing that eventually makes you attractive. That is what becomes your platform. It makes you stand out, and people are attracted to you. But it depends significantly on how you react to pain.

The Apostle Paul said there is indeed a connection between pain and grace.[8] I pray for you, as you read this book, that God will resolve in your life the things that only God can resolve. I pray that your testimonies will be the types that will make you stand out. I believe so strongly that God will turn your circumstances around, and everything that has tested you will become a testimony.

I want you to know that the very things that have caused me to shed tears in the past are now the things that form the core of my messages. In fact, they are the very reason

---

8 2 Corinthians 1:9

why people want to listen to me. I have been denied visas, suffered extreme poverty, been stuck on a low-paying job, looked with longing eyes at beautiful things knowing that I could not afford them. I have lived in shame. I have been treated with spite simply because of my financial status. However, things have changed, and now people want to hear my story. Can you imagine that? Can you see the relationship between pain and grace? I declare this to you: You are a candidate for grace!

Change your Focus

Be encouraged, dear friend. Stop giving pain all your attention because as long as you do that, you will become bitter. Bitterness is a poison of grace. Grace cannot work in the life of a bitter person because it is faith that activates grace. Remember what Jesus said. He declared, "You have something against your brother and you come to the altar to make a sacrifice, go back and settle with your brother. If you don't forgive your brother, your father in heaven will not forgive you."[9]

The truth is that "God will not allow you to be tempted above what can bear, but he will make a way of escape."[10] The keyword here is "allow." God is ever-present, and He is aware of every situation. Whatever you seek is what you will find. If you keep your focus on the source of pain, especially when it is a human being, it will make you bitter. Change your focus.

I learned many years ago that no matter how dark the cloud might be, it will surely pass and the sun will still shine. God is the one who has power over the clouds, so keep your focus

9 Matthew 5:23-24
10 1 Corinthians 10:3

on God. With this assurance, you can walk around full of confidence and joy. Focus on God, who does not change, not the circumstances that are in your face. I guarantee you that as long as your focus is on God, you will receive His grace.

Years ago, each time I was refused a visa. I grew more and more bitter with the officers at the embassy. I can only imagine how many people have sent curses their way. Some of them had already developed a notorious reputation for denying visas. You see, we often need a target to point our bitterness at, and in this case, we believe it was the devil and that one visa officer. After all the denials, I remember going to the embassy one day, and as I sat down waiting my turn, a voice said in my heart that I would not receive the visa. I prayed. I said, "Lord, if I don't get this visa here today, then I would know it is You." I had prayed, fasted, and "binded and casted" in the spirit before coming. I had done everything humanly possible, so I was sure that no devil could deny me. If I was denied this time, it had to be God standing in my way.

I had prayed so much, I was sure that every devil in my way left, so who was left? You see, that's the problem with

so many of us. We can't see God's hand until all the demons are "out of the way." When I got to the officer, I was denied. But this time, and for the very first time, I left the embassy without any bitterness or malice. It can be painful and traumatic, but I walked out smiling. I do not know why, but I felt free inside. I was free because, for the first time, I was looking at God, not my pain or rejection.

Let me repeat it. When you are focused on God, you know that the situation is not your end. In all your circumstances,

God always has the last word; and that is why you can rejoice! You can relax. After that experience, I asked God, "Lord! What is it? What do you want me to do?" And I heard Him say, "That's it! That is what I have been waiting for you to say all this while." That was when everything changed. Now, my visa denial days are a testimony because God turned it all around.

Progress in the Process

I also remember when I was frustrated with the rate at which our church was growing. It was so frustrating that I had started questioning if I was even supposed to be pastoring. Things simply weren't going the way I had expected. I asked my dear wife, Nike, to come along on a retreat to seek the face of the Lord because I needed to be sure I had heard God correctly about starting a church. I told Him, "I don't want to waste my life. Am I supposed to be pastoring at all?"

I also went to speak to my pastor, and I will never forget his words of encouragement and the scripture he shared with me. He shared a scripture with me saying, *"Let us not be weary in well doing, in due season, we shall reap if we faint not."*[11] He told me to keep doing what we were doing. You see, harvests are seasonal. Things will definitely change in due course of time. It is a principle. For a few months, mostly on Saturdays, we had been holding management meetings trying to find a winning strategy to increase our membership. We had been searching tirelessly for a new location for our services, and even when we would find a place we liked, we would not have the resources to get it.

A few months later, I had a dream that was so vivid it had to be a vision. I saw a new auditorium for our church. I

---

11 Galatians 6:9

saw my pastor, Dr. David Oyedepo, and his wife, coming to visit in the dream. It was so clear and detailed. They arrived in an SUV and my wife and I received them. He then returned to the car and came out with a plant that had leaves, planted it in the soil, and began to prophesy. As he did, people suddenly began running towards us and within a few minutes, a large crowd had gathered around. Next, we went to inspect the new auditorium, and I saw a man speaking using a microphone at one end and a lady at the other end, speaking to another group of people. Afterward, my pastor and his wife drove off, and then ministry friends from the city began to shake hands with my wife and myself, congratulating us on what had happened. That was when I woke up, and I immediately knew that there had been a shift in the spirit realm.

After that powerful dream, only a few weeks later, I got a book titled Purpose Driven Church by Rick Warren. I immediately called our pastors to an all-night meeting because everyone was so agitated by the lack of growth. I told them about the book and read the first chapter, and we began to discuss how the book applied to our church, Daystar Christian Center. From the moment I started reading, I can tell you that someone else took over that meeting. The Holy Spirit took over! The outcome of that meeting was beyond anything any of us had envisaged, and the rest is history. People often ask how we did it, but honestly, how do you answer that? Grace was activated. What we did that produced results came after what God did!

I pray that God will interrupt your life, and you will see the clear distinction of this dimension of grace. You will receive what you thought you were never qualified to receive. You will sit with people that you've only seen on TV. You will receive job offers beyond your wildest imagination. Expect a miracle because grace is being activated in your life right now!

Trust God's Process

Remember that it is important how you manage what is missing in your life. Take note of how you react to the source of pain. The starting point is to speak to God and give Him your total trust. In fact, I remember God telling me once, "The day you fight with someone for leaving this church, it will be proof of your belief that I am weak. Don't try it!" That's why you can't afford to be bitter about anyone or any painful situation because that will be proof of your lack of trust and faith in God's ability to change the situation. Instead, expect the grace of God to work. It works!

Remember what Job said amid his pain? "Though he slays me, yet I will trust him."[12] Let go and let God. Declare your absolute trust in God. There is no point in trying to change what you cannot change. Leave God to change it in style. Solomon said, "Trust in the Lord with all your heart, lean not on your own understanding, in all your ways acknowledge

Him, recognize Him, He is there; He said He will direct your steps."[13]

Unleash the Weapon of Joy

Apostle Paul said, "I rejoice in my infirmities." Grace is activated when you can rejoice amid adversity. Your help comes from the Lord, the God who made heaven and earth. He will not suffer my foot to be moved, He who keeps Israel will not cause me to stumble. How powerful is that! You

---

12 Job 13:15
13 Proverbs 3:5-6

must stop being desperate and quit trying to manipulate your circumstances! Grace is what makes the difference.

There is indeed a wellspring of grace, and I see it pouring out over you. No mountain can stand before you. Grace is activated in your life. Only grace can level mountains. Just give God praise because the things that are impossible with men are possible with God. Step into the realm of possibilities, which is the realm of grace. The pain you are going through is proof that you are a candidate for grace.

CHAPTER

3

Connecting
with Grace

"Not by power nor by might"

It takes grace to do things that are beyond human ability. Grace is simply divine power made available to carry out God's purposes on the earth. The truth is that everyone living on divine purpose will eventually attract opposition. The devil stands against the will of God on this planet. This is why it is critical to be connected to the grace of God. It is that connection that defeats the purpose of the enemy in your life.

Zechariah had a vision in the Bible. It reads, "Now the angel who talked with me came back and wakened me as a man who is wakened out of his sleep, and he said to me, "what do you see?" So I said, "I am looking, and there is a lampstand of solid gold with a bowl on top of it, and on the stand seven lamps with seven pipes to the seven lamps. Two olive trees are by it, one at the right of the bowl and the other at its left." So I answered and spoke to the angel who talked with me saying, " what are these, my lord?" Then the angel who talked with me answered and said to me, "do you not know what these are?" And I said, "No, my lord." So he answered and said to me: "this is the word of the Lord to Zerubbabel: 'Not by power nor by might, but by my Spirit' says the Lord of hosts. 'Who are you, o great mountain? Before Zerubbabel, you shall become a plain."[1]

According to the angel, the two olive trees, on either side of the lampstand, are the two anointed ones. The ones who stand beside the Lord of the whole earth. You see, the opposition that Zerubbabel was facing was fierce. He had been tasked with building the temple of God, and it had taken years to make any progress. The opposition was so bad that they were forced to stop building. It seemed like an impossible situation, but God spoke to His prophet, Zechariah.

The word of the Lord came saying, "This is the word of the Lord to Zerubbabel: 'Not by power nor by might, but by my Spirit says the Lord of hosts. 'Who are you, O great mountain? Before Zerubbabel, you shall become a plain." Later on, God said, "the hands of Zerubbabel have laid the foundation of this temple; his hands shall also finish it. Then you will know that the Lord of hosts has sent me to you."[2]

---

1 Zechariah 4:1-7
2 Zechariah 4:9

The Power to deal with Delay and Denial

Everything that God has designed to be part of your destiny that has stopped working, I pray that there is a reactivation of grace in those areas of your life right now. That is what grace is all about. Grace is what turns impossibilities to possibilities. It is God's memo of speed and access to any delay or denial that we face. When Ezra led the captives back from Babylon, they started the audacious project of rebuilding the temple, but the Samaritans launched threats and attacks against them. Zechariah and Haggai, the prophets of God, were God's mouthpiece as the people immediately began to pray. They prophesied, "Who are you mountain that stands before Zerubbabel? You will become a plain. And I will bring out of that mountain that is disturbing him a cornerstone, and he will be shouting grace! grace! grace!"[3]

Anyone who is out to fulfill the purpose of God will attract opposition from the devil. Some of us don't even understand the reason why we are going through what we are going through. But I guarantee you one thing, you stand with God, you stay with God, through thick and thin, and tomorrow you will look back and understand why. You will discover that it is about the value of your destiny.

The devil wouldn't waste his time on you if you didn't have an amazing destiny ahead of you. Some years ago, my health broke down due to stress, and I was admitted to the hospital. While I was there, I drifted off into sleep and had a spiritual encounter. I remember quite clearly that it was in the afternoon and I saw a woman who had just delivered a baby.

---

3 Zechariah 4:6

Suddenly, I saw demons, emitting black smoke, coming to take that baby away. I immediately grabbed the baby from the woman and ran. While running, I came across a wide gorge, a really deep pit in my path. Behind me, the swarm of evil chased after me. I decided to leap across, and halfway, I realized that there was absolutely no way that I would make it across. I immediately cried out to God for help, and He did! God's hand appeared and lifted me up, with the baby in my arms, and placed me on the other side. The interesting thing is that the black smoke of the demons appeared again, but this time I opened my mouth and shouted loud and clear, "In the Name of Jesus Christ!" The next thing, I woke up!

That spiritual experience had seemed like it took a while, but in reality, I had just been lying on the hospital bed for a few minutes. But things were just getting started. Not long after, I drifted again into sleep, and the next moment, I saw myself at an African country, where a massive crowd had gathered singing praises and worshiping God in African attire. The next moment, I found myself in another African country, with another massive crowd standing in front of me in their different attires. That was when I understood what was going on. It was because I was carrying something precious that the enemy was coming after me in the revelation.

I pray for you that whatever it is that the devil is afraid of about you, God will surely make that thing happen in the name of Jesus Christ. When I look back now, I understand now with absolute clarity why the devil wanted to take me out in that revelation. I see now why he has challenged me every step of the way. You know, while I was in college, the devil would cut my finances. I was so broke I didn't have anything to eat. Now, I understand why. The devil was trying so hard to ruin me, to make me stay in poverty.

Your Destiny is the Target

Think about Joseph in the Bible. His destiny was such a threat to the devil that he was almost killed. You may think your problems are because of a poor education or where you were born. Listen, friend. It's way bigger than that. The devil does not like your destiny. If he had his way, he would take your life. I am so glad, and you should rejoice that there's absolutely nothing he can do to stop a person connected to grace.

Yes! Hallelujah! I'm telling you that if he could have killed you, he would have done so already. My mother had a child before I was born, who died three days after his birth. When I was born, they named me Samuel, which means "God heard" or, "I asked of him from the Lord." I am still here today! If he could not kill me, then, it is too late now. I am connected to grace.

Zerubbabel's mission attracted opposition because he was building God's temple. He had a powerful calling and still had to deal with delay. There are so many out there in the world who seem to be prospering but are already ruined. That is why it is so unwise and faithless to envy others, not to mention envying people who do not believe in God. It's like being concerned about someone eating food and drinking all the wine on a sinking ship. Who cares about all that when the ship is sinking? That is why the devil isn't bothered about them and is more focused on a Child of God whose life is on-mission.

Let me tell you this. If the devil is coming after you, rejoice!

You are connected to grace. There is indeed something special about your destiny. Someone said, "I don't understand what's going on. Before I got saved, everything was going just fine. Now, it seems like things aren't working out for me. Is it that God is not working on my behalf?" My response is that you are on the right track. The devil is afraid of your destiny.

Zerubbabel and the people of Judah experienced opposition firsthand. "Then the people of the land tried to discourage the people of Judah. They troubled them in building, and hired counselors against them to frustrate their purpose all the days of Cyrus king of Persia, even until the reign of Darius king of Persia."[4] Isn't that remarkable? They had to hire people to help them.

Something remarkable happened afterwards because the prophets Haggai and Zechariah prophesied to the Jews who were in Judah and Jerusalem, and work started again. Zerubbabel, the son of Shealtiel and Jeshua the son of Jozadak, rose up and began to build the house of God, which was in Jerusalem; and the prophets of God were with them helping them.[5] When the prophets of God came on the scene, things started working again. "Not by power nor by might, but by my spirit," says the Lord of hosts.

The Missing Ingredient

I had an experience as a young Christian. I used to attend every Christian event in town, every seminar, and every conference. I would feel so supercharged each time like fully loaded with power to cast out demons and raise the dead. But three days after the event, I would feel like I was back

---

4 Ezra 4:4-5
5 Ezra 5:1&2

to square one. The euphoria of the event would fade away until I attended the next one. When you go through this cycle consistently, you end up fatigued. The truth is that it's about understanding the power in the prophetic. That is what makes the difference. When God's word is released, suffering meets its end. Peter told Jesus, "Master, we have toiled all night, we have taken nothing, but nevertheless, at your word…"[6]

When the word of God is missing from your life, you lose your identity, because the proof of His presence and grace will disappear. When prophecy ceases, signs, and wonders go on vacation. Everything grinds to a standstill when the ministry of prophecy isn't available. The prophetic connects you to grace. Remember that signs are proof of God's grace in your life. You should be concerned if all that is happening in your life is by the power of a human being.

In the Bible, Jehoshaphat went before God and cried out. He said, "We do not have the power to handle this great multitude and we don't even know what to do. What should we do?"[7] Then, a prophet came on the scene and said, "Hold on Jehoshaphat! Thus saith the Lord, you will not need to fight in this battle." Stand still! Remain steadfast. The Lord, your God, will fight for you; you will not have to do anything." Upon hearing those words from the prophet, Jehoshaphat stood before the people, who were discouraged and overwhelmed, and announced, "Believe the Lord your God and you will be established. Believe also His prophets and you will prosper!" [8]

---

6 Luke 5:5
7 2 Chronicles 20:12
8 2 Chronicles 20:20

The Most Valuable Commodity

The most valuable commodity on planet earth isn't rubies, money or diamonds. It is, "Thus says the Lord." The word of God is the power that rules the universe. If you want to be connected to God's grace, you must be desperate for the word of God. Be hungry for it! I'm not talking about reading the Bible like a novel. I'm talking about being desperate for a personal word from God.

There's something about a prophet who carries the grace of God. It is grace that is transferable. It flows over into your life and creates the atmosphere for you to hear the word of God for yourself. I remember listening to Dr. David Oyedepo's tapes every day back then. I would play and replay his messages in my car. It became a habit. I often wondered where he got his deep insights. Then one day, it hit me. I had been listening to his message, and then I opened my Bible. The first page I opened, a revelation just unraveled right in front of me. I received a powerful and deep insight. I realized at that moment that I had received the grace of God on Dr. Oyedepo's life, and it was making me gain insights from the scriptures like him.

The Bible was written under the anointing, and it takes the anointing to understand it. "For I commend you to God and to the word of His grace which is able to build you up and to give you an inheritance among those who are sanctified."[9] This is indeed your season of revelation. You will receive revelation, and it will produce signs of grace in your life. Just believe it.

What about the widow who was in a desperate financial situation? Her two sons were about to be taken away as slaves.

---

9 Acts 20:32

Can you imagine that? But she ran to a prophet. It's time you stop running to your friends or social media. It's time you stop running back and forth. It's time to run to God, the source of revelation. This widow ran to the prophet, and he asked her, "What do you have in your house?" She responded that she had a small jar of oil. He then told her to go quickly and borrow empty vessels. Now, that would obviously seem like a ridiculous instruction. But she believed the prophet, ran, and acted on his instructions, pouring her small jar of oil into the borrowed vessels. The oil did not stop flowing until she had filled up every single borrowed vessel. She received revelation, and poverty was terminated.

Now, I am not encouraging you to run all over the place, looking for people to instruct you. The structure under the new covenant is different from that of the old covenant. You have the Holy Spirit inside you now to teach you all things. We still have prophets in the new covenant, and God uses them to speak into our lives. More of than not, though, they confirm what God has impressed on our hearts already. Don't abdicate the responsibly for hearing from God.

God has destined the end of lack in your life as you read this book. You are receiving revelation for your next level. The prophetic word carries God's solution to the challenges we face. There are countless stories to share. There was the woman who had no child who gave lodging to the prophet, Elisha. One day, the prophetic word came, and it turned the impossible situation in her life around. She gave birth to a son because she believed that word. I pray for you that whatever barrenness you are experiencing ends today has come to an end. I prophesy over you that those who mocked you will be the first to see the explosive power of God at work in your life.

CHAPTER

4

Prayer, Access to Grace

"You do not have because you do not ask."

Grace is simply God's undeserved gift. The Christian life has been designed by God to be lived by grace. Even our salvation, priceless and requiring the ultimate sacrifice, was given to us by grace. Grace is a gift. This revelation will change your life. For by grace, you have been saved through faith, and that not of yourselves; it is the gift of God. [1] Salvation is not from our works. We would never work hard enough to earn it. It is a precious gift.

---

1 Ephesians 2:8

Works in this context refer to human effort. So there's an apparent dilemma. How you operate in the realm of salvation by grace but run your life by works? When God starts something in our lives by grace, isn't it absurd to attempt completing it by works? The scriptures say that, "Being confident of this very thing, that He who has begun a good work in you will complete it until the day of Jesus Christ."[2] Another verse says, "for it is God who works in you both to will and to do for His good pleasure."[3] You see, our lives are to be lived by His grace, by God's divine ability.

A Life Lived by Grace

It's amazing that even with our knowledge of God's desire to bless us, many Christians keep trying to be blessed by relying on their own "intelligence." This is pride, and the Bible says that the grace that God gives is stronger, and God resists the proud but gives grace to the humble.[4] A proud person is someone who is trying to run their own life on their own. The humble person acknowledges the need for God's help. God can work unhindered in the life of a humble person, but the proud person's resistance will come from God himself.

I discovered something about Jesus, and that is He lived by grace. The scriptures say, "And the child grew, and became strong in spirit, filled with wisdom: and the grace of God was upon him."[5] Isn't it interesting that we think that the grace came upon Jesus after He was baptized at the river Jordan. We assume that this was the first time the Holy Spirit's anointing would come upon Him. Well, we now

---

2 Philippians 1:6
3 Philippians 2:13
4 James 4:6
5 Luke 2:40

know that Jesus had been enjoying God's grace since He was a child. In fact, the grace of God has been with Him since He was in the womb conceived by the Holy Spirit.

Jesus was conceived by grace and born by grace. The Word became flesh and made His dwelling among us. We have seen His glory, the glory of the one and only Son, who came from the Father, full of grace and truth.[6] Out of His fullness, we have all received grace in place of grace already given. For the law was given through Moses; grace and truth came through Jesus Christ.[7] So, what Jesus received at the River Jordan was divine empowerment for serving others, but all His life, He had learned how to live with the power of God daily. We need to learn this too.

Most times, we focus on the miracles that happened in the ministry of Jesus, but we often miss out on His lifestyle. Jesus had a lifestyle of prayer, of absolute and total dependence on God. From the scriptures, we understand that Jesus stripped Himself of all power and authority and came purely as a human being to the earth. So while He was on earth, He needed God's help though He was the second person of the trinity. Jesus did this so he could experience the human condition, embracing our humanity fully. That's why prayer was a top priority for Jesus. It provided the access He needed to have the power of God surging through His life daily.

There is a verse of scripture that provides some insight into the prayer life of Jesus. It says, "In the days of his flesh, when he had offered prayers and supplications, with vehement cries and tears to him who was able to save him from death and was heard because of His godly fear, though He was God's

---

6 John 1:14
7 John 1:16

Son, he learned trusting-obedience by the things which he suffered."[8] This makes it clear that it was His dependence on God that led Him to pray. This is the secret ingredient that produces access to the grace of God.

There is an internal battle that we all face. James painted the perfect picture when he wrote, "You lust and do not have. You murder and covet and cannot obtain it. You fight and war, yet you do not have because you do not ask."[9] It is the kind of war that you fight when you struggle with anxiety and worry. It is battling against the apprehension that comes from envisioning the future when things are out of control. It is the battle that comes from fighting against manipulation, against contention. It is the internal strife that comes from either choosing to trust God or to trust in one's abilities. It's a war!

Grace is Free

When you come across a Christian who lives by works, who thinks he or she is smart enough to run his or her own life, you have come across a person whose prayer life is shallow. Whether they know it or not, they have decided internally that they don't need God. God allows us to face challenges so we can recognize our need for Him. It is in our weaknesses and challenges that we see the power of grace when we abandon our dependence on self and cling to the grace that God gives so freely.

The Apostle Paul, as we discussed in Chapter 2, described how he had to contend with a messenger of Satan sent to harass him so he would not get into pride due to the abundance of revelation that had been given to him. He sought the face

8 Hebrews 5:7
9 James 4:2

of the Lord concerning this "thorn in his flesh" three times and then, God responded, saying, "My grace is sufficient for you."[10] In other words, God was telling him, "I won't remove the problem. But I will give you grace." Why? It was God's opportunity to pour out His grace upon Paul.

There is no way that grace can be activated in the life of a Christian who thinks he or she does not need God. These are the types of believers who try to pay for something that God has labeled a gift. They are wired to pay to get and pay to play, but the blessings of the Christian faith are products of the free gift of grace. How powerful this verse of scripture is: For you know the grace of our Lord Jesus Christ, that though He was rich, yet for your sakes He became poor, that you through His poverty might become rich.[11] This makes it abundantly clear that prosperity is a product of grace, not sweat.

Prayer is the Key

The challenge that Paul was facing drove him to God, and God was happy for him to stay that way. Could it be that what you are fighting is the only reason you have fellowship with God? The greater the challenges we face, the greater the grace we encounter when we run to God. Prayer is all about fellowshipping with God. It is beyond an activity; rather, it is about communion. God simply wants to spend quality time with us.

The scriptures say, "Now in the morning, having risen a long while before daylight, He went out and departed to a solitary place, and there He prayed."[12] Jesus spent quality time with God, but we have turned prayer into work.

---

10 2 Corinthians 12:9
11 2 Corinthians 8:9
12 Mark 1:35

Just because we have read that Jesus would stay all night on a mountain to pray, we have made a doctrine out of all-night prayers. Some have come to believe that God's blessing is a reward for the length of time they dedicate to prayer. Sorry to burst your bubble, but that can't be further from the truth. You can never qualify for God's blessings that way. You can never pay for it. It is a gift. Your focus should be on communion, which should dictate how much time you spend, rather than laboring in works and hoping that God rewards you for the amount of time spent.

God sees beyond our dramatic expressions in prayer. Just be yourself, whether you're an extrovert or introvert, express yourself and be real with God. God has the capacity not only to hear the words of your mouth, but the words of your mind as well. He is able to do exceedingly abundantly above all you can ask or think.[13] Spend quality time in communion with God, not out of works, but from your heart because He loves you and wants to be close to you always.

Remember this: it is when we accept our inability to fulfill our own destiny that we recognize our deep need for prayers. Spend time in fellowship with God, and you will soon come to understand what grace means. David was one of those that understood this powerful secret. He was just an ordinary shepherd boy, and while everyone else was going about their important businesses, he was in the fields taking care of sheep. He was often alone with no one to talk to, and in that process, he discovered he could communicate with the invisible God. Being the one designated to take care of sheep must have seemed like a disadvantage. It was the work no one else wanted to do, and yet it became a tremendous blessing for him. Sometimes, it's the very people around us

13 Ephesians 3:20

who provide support that make us miss out on God. We have become over-reliant on our connections, our power network, or our wealthy family members.

I think it's easier for those who have no earthly helper to discover the power of prayer quickly. Here was a young David, alone with sheep, and a distance away from home and comfort, but that was where he learned to play an instrument of worship. I can assure you starting a new relationship can be very awkward. It's because it takes time to develop intimacy. It can even feel more awkward to be alone in a room with an invisible God, but I tell you this, if you continue, you will develop intimacy and experience the sweetness of God. You get to taste and see that the Lord is good.

There is no human fellowship that compares with fellowshipping with God. You can't remain the same when you fellowship with Him. It is impossible. The more David discovered God, the more assured he became about life. He learned so much from his extensive time of fellowship with God that he discovered peace, safety, and absolute trust in God. The reason why we struggle with anxiety is that we don't know God. Those who know their God will be strong, and they will do exploits.[14] The more you know God, the more faith you will have. Situations and circumstances that have stood as a challenge will fade because you will come to realize those seemingly insurmountable issues are away too small for God. You will see things from God's perspective.

Revelation Comes Through Prayer

The problem you are facing becomes the greatest opportunity of your life when you begin to see things from

---

14 Daniel 11:32

God's perspective. As you stay in the place of communion and fellowship with God, you will experience a revelation. David began to receive revelation as he spent time with God. In fact, he was one of the few who received prophetic insight into the coming of the Savior. Some of David's prophecies are:

Sacrifice and offering You did not desire, but a body You have prepared for Me. In burnt offerings and sacrifices for sin You had no pleasure. Then I said, 'Behold, I have come—In the volume of the book it is written of Me—To do Your will, O God. [15]

He was prophesying about Christ. "The Lord said to my Lord, "Sit at My right hand till I make Your enemies Your footstool."" [16]

Your throne, O God, is forever and ever; A scepter of righteousness is the scepter of Your kingdom. You love righteousness and hate wickedness; Therefore God, Your God, has anointed You with the oil of gladness more than Your companions. [17]

Wow! David knew God! He received a depth of access into the heart of God. When God was looking for a king to rule over Israel, after His rejection of King Saul, God picked this young man from the fields. He was anointed with oil because God knew that ruling Israel needed more than human ability. He needed someone who knew how to activate grace to lead His people. David was not in the royal lineage, but God changed the order. I see God creating new power structures to elevate you.

---

15 Hebrews 10:5-7
16 Psalm 110:1
17 Psalm 45:6-7

One other person who fellowshipped greatly with God, and who really challenged me is Moses. Moses communed with God. What most of us do is talk. We talk and talk and never take time to listen. How can you be intimate with someone and always do all the talking? That means you don't really know the person. Prayer isn't just about talking; it's even more about listening.

A Two-Way Exchange

When I was courting my wife, she would mostly do the talking, and I think she realized that one day. I remember picking her up from work to give her a ride to her home, and the car was so quiet. I realized she wasn't saying much. She had deliberately decided not to say anything because she wanted me to talk. That was the day I realized how bad a conversationalist I was. When she did the talking, it was just okay, but now, I had the pressure of bringing up topics for conversation. After that day, anytime I was going to see her, I would prepare five topics in advance. We started talking more and more, even trivial issues.

That's how you figure out more about the other person. It's not just all about the serious conversations. Tell God exactly how you feel. David wasn't afraid to tell God when he was angry. When he was afraid, he didn't try to hide that. When he felt like God had abandoned him, he told God that. That is communion. It's time to go beyond mechanical prayers to communion. No devil can make a failure out of a person who stays in constant communion with God.

Look at what Moses did. Moses took his tent and pitched it outside the camp, far from the camp, and called it the tabernacle of meeting. And it came to pass that everyone who sought the Lord went out to the tabernacle of meeting, which was outside the camp.[18] Take note, Moses took his tent, his own tent. He separated himself, and his tent became a place where he met with God.

Whenever Moses went out to the tabernacle, all the people rose, and each person stood at his tent door and watched Moses until he had gone into the tabernacle. When Moses entered the tabernacle, the pillar of cloud descended and stood at the door of the tabernacle, and the Lord talked with Moses. All the people saw the pillar of cloud standing at the tabernacle door, and all the people rose and worshiped, each man in his tent door.[19] Wow! Anytime Moses went into the tent, the people came out and watched, knowing that something was about to happen.

Many people hang around men of God and prophets, but they never discover their secret. They attempt to replicate works and decisions and miss out on the secret. Only one man figured out Moses' secret. That was Joshua. You see, every time Moses went out, Joshua went with him. He sat down and observed Moses in communion with God. There is a particular account shared about how Joshua stayed back in the tabernacle when Moses was done. Joshua must have wanted to experience deep communion like Moses and began to develop a personal relationship as well. No surprise that when it was time to pick a successor, no one else was qualified before God save Joshua. Moses skipped many older, more experienced leaders because he knew that it would take grace to lead such a powerful nation.

It is the grace of God that counts, and Moses understood this. Moses said, "See, You say to me, 'Bring up these people.'

18 Exodus 33:7
19 Exodus 33:10

But You have not let me know whom You will send with me. Yet You have said, 'I know you by name, and you have also found grace in My sight.' Now, therefore, I pray, if I have found grace in Your sight, show me now Your way, that I may know You and that I may find grace in Your sight. And consider that this nation is Your people."[20] This was Moses, who had witnessed the parting of the red sea. He had seen water coming out of a rock. He had seen so many amazing signs and wonders in Egypt, and regardless of all of that, he still wanted to "know God more."

I pray we can get to that level of absolute dependence on God, where we say, "If God does not go with us, then we're calling off this trip or project." If you want to live an extraordinary life, then you need to be through trying to run your own life and trust God all the way. Moses was so close to God that he asked God to show him His glory. That is the depth of intimacy; when you say, "I want to see you." This is the type of closeness and fellowship I want with God. Moses had such an amazing encounter with God, and it changed him. When he came down from the mountain after speaking to God, there was light all over his face, and the people were afraid.

The more communion you have with God, the more you are changed and transformed. God rubs off on you. I pray that you as you trust God more, you will receive access to deeper levels of grace. Expect miracles of grace. God will do exceedingly and abundantly more than you can ask or think.

---

20 Exodus 13:12

5

Grace and your Assignment

"This mountain will become a plain."

In this chapter, my focus will be on helping you understand the relationship between grace and your divine assignment. Think about the Apostles and the early church. It is written about them that "…with great power the apostles gave witness to the resurrection of the Lord Jesus. And great grace was upon them all."[1] You see! There are realms and levels of power, but accessing great power requires great grace working in your life. No one can refute the evidence of grace in your life. It will leave your enemies in wonder, and people around you will give glory to God.

---

1 Acts 4:33

The Pharisees did everything they could to shut down the apostles, but they even had to admit that a notable miracle had been done, and there was no way they could deny it. I pray for you that you will receive a notable miracle from God in the name of Jesus Christ. Amen.

Grace for Divine Direction

Everyone on-assignment needs a clear direction. In the mission field of life, you need a clear path ahead of you. The first thing you enjoy when the grace of God is upon your life is direction. God always makes known His will, giving us a clear direction. When we obey His directives, things work. While others are relying on human intelligence to figure things out, you have the voice of the Holy Spirit. That's why one right step in the path of divine direction results in giant leaps because the calculations, permutations, and combinations activated in the spirit by grace are more sophisticated than human intelligence.

There is no amount of talent, gift, or skill that eliminates the need for grace. Grace is God's divine influence on display in your life. It is walking in the realm of results beyond human abilities. When God's grace is at work in your life, the evidence is undeniable. No obstacle can withstand the power of grace. I strongly believe that as you read this chapter, you will experience transformation, the type of transformation that will herald the mighty acts of God in your life. Frustrations will put in their resignation letters, and you will make progress.

You see, each one of us has a unique calling from God, a mandate that He has given to us to fulfill His purpose on the earth. I have seen greatly talented men and women of God run on empty. I have seen passionate youth end up in frustration. The common denominator was that they abandoned grace and focused on human strategies and human thinking. There are so many scenarios where people attempt to take control of the steering wheel of their own lives. We attempt to be successful in our marriages, raising children, prospering in our careers, or building successful businesses with our own power. I know what it is like to make some money with and without the grace of God. There is a clear difference.

Grace for Divine Relationships

I know what it's like for God to be involved. When God is involved, things will happen that you did not have any hand in. Your smartness will look like foolishness compared to the doors that grace will open. Grace turns you into a magnet of goodness. You will begin to see things flowing into your life, things you know you have no power to attract. It is the abundant grace of God that attracts those things to you. I have seen people graced to have friends who they are not naturally qualified to be in the same circle with.

God can bless you with divine relationships. This is just a byproduct of grace. Not by power, not by might, but by Spirit says the Lord. At the end of human ability resides the manifold beauty of God's grace. Can you imagine what life would be like when mountains can no longer stand in front of you; when poverty stays far away from you? You can't be graced and be broke. In fact, I pray that fear fades away, and you begin to walk in the confidence that only God can give. Grace gives the devil boundaries because he realizes that God has taken the wheel.

Grace for Divine Doors

Another thing that I love about grace is that it leaps over your calculations. You can plot the graph of your purpose, set your goals, and use all the project management skills you have learned, but I have realized that too much calculation leads to frustration, and too much analysis leads to paralysis. It's time you activated grace. It is allowing the God who calls those things there are not as though they were into the equation. Difficult things become easy when grace is in action.

There was a young man who needed a job that attended a crusade. During the crusade, there was a prayer call for everyone to pray about their needs. He began to pray, just like everyone else around him. Unknown to him, someone was standing close by who had a business. The person, in the middle of prayer, heard the voice of the Holy Spirit to offer the young man a job. That was it! The business owner walked up to the young man and asked, "Do you need a job?" They conducted the interview right there in the middle of prayer on a crusade ground. Total strangers brought together by grace.

It's that simple. We're the ones who over-complicate everything when grace is available to make things simple. It's like stocking up dynamite to blow up a mountain. How long will it take and how much? God said, "I will make this mountain a plain." Leave the "figuring it out" to God. God's grace is beyond human technology and techniques.

Grace for Abundance

There was a time that Isaac wanted to go down to Egypt, but God said, "Stay right where you are. Stay and just obey my voice and I will bless you."[2] Do you know that Isaac obeyed,

---

2 Genesis 26:2

sowed in that land and reaped a hundredfold. He was so blessed where he was that the Philistines envied him. This is the power of grace at work.

We also see this grace at work in the life of Jacob. Jacob had a very difficult employer who also happened to be his uncle, Laban. Laban was so terrible that he reviewed Jacob's wages downward ten times, yet with all that, Jacob still left Laban's house more prosperous than Laban. This is grace at work.

We see grace at work in the life of Joseph. Although he was sold into slavery, Joseph prospered and was successful even as a slave in Potiphar's house. The hand of God was on him. In fact, no one would have remembered Potiphar in history, if not for Joseph. In fact, it is written that Potiphar recognized that God was with Joseph.[3]

Grace was also at work in the life of Moses. Can you imagine one man confronting the global power that Egypt was back then? He stood against the pharaoh, and crippled the entire economy. It was the power of God upon His life. He led out an entire nation out of slavery and led them through dry land amid the Red Sea. God brought about wonders through his mouth and staff. It is grace.

Jesus, himself, was full of grace. He went to the river Jordan to be baptized, and the heavens opened over Him. There's a remarkable account of Jesus going to the temple after the power of the Spirit had come upon Him. He went to the front of the temple and read the scriptures from the scroll. The people just stared at Him in wonder at the gracious words that proceeded from his lips. There was something different about Him this time. It was grace at work.

---

3 Genesis 39:3

What do we say about the Disciples of Christ? A collection of fishermen, tax collectors, and other professions, who were living ordinary lives until they met Christ. They spoke in languages they never knew before, healed the sick, and raised the dead. That was grace at work.

I can assure you that your words will move this world once you walk in grace. God's word in your mouth will be as powerful as God's word in God's mouth! Your words will create and recreate. Your words will bring healing and restoration. The Bible says that Jesus cast out spirits through His words.[4] The spirit world is moved by words. Angels respond to words. When the grace of God is upon your life, your words are filled with power.

Grace and your Calling

Grace is given for the fulfillment of an assignment. God always gives grace and His power for the fulfillment of a calling. You locate your grace in the place of your assignment. And it is important to note: Your assignment is not in your decision, it is in your revelation. Apostle, Paul made it clear that he did not receive his assignment from any human being. He had an encounter with God that changed his testimony. Apostle Paul wrote, "But I make known to you, brethren that the gospel which was preached by me is not according to man. For I neither received it from man, nor was I taught it, but it came through the revelation of Jesus Christ. For you have heard of my former conduct in Judaism, how I persecuted the church of God beyond measure and tried to destroy it. And I advanced in Judaism beyond many of my contemporaries in my own nation, being more exceedingly zealous for the traditions of the fathers. But when it pleased

---

4 Matthew 8:16

God, who separated me from my mother's womb and called me through His grace, to reveal His Son in me, that I might preach Him among the Gentiles, I did not immediately confer with flesh and blood, nor did I go up to Jerusalem to those who were apostles before me; but I went to Arabia, and returned again to Damascus."[5]

I love that! Every Christian should have a personal testimony. No one can teach you your assignment. In life, some things can be taught, and some other things caught. Apostle Paul caught the revelations he received in the realm of the Spirit. There is no human guide, coach, or counselor that was there when God designed your destiny. Remember all I have written about communion? Getting revelation from God is a product of communion, your personal fellowship with God.

You have "caught it" when you can confidently declare that God told you or that God led you. For me, I can confidently tell you what God wants me to do with my life. I was a student in college when I listened to a sermon preached from the Book of Luke chapter 12 verse 24, which reads, "For where your treasure is, there your heart will be also." I remember getting back to my room and praying, "Lord, show me where You have put my treasure in life, so that I can put my heart there." I said, "Lord, I don't want to waste my life. Show me where my treasure is so that I can put my heart there." It was only a few days after when I found the answer. It was an impression on my heart: "You will be a preacher, not a contractor."

I was being groomed to become a contractor so I could take over my father's company. Just like Apostle Paul said, that

---

5 Galatians 1:11-17

he had been very busy doing what he was good at, he had excelled beyond everyone else in his pursuit of his passion for Judaism. He had become notorious for imprisoning Christians. But when God stopped him in his tracks, he was aligned with his divine assignment. I had a similar experience. My family had a plan crafted out for me; it was a family plan. My grandfather was a builder. In fact, he was the head of the builders in our village, and my father took up the family profession. He was a builder and contractor. I was in my second year of high school when my name was added to the directors list of the company. At that age, I was already a director, and I was so excited about the future that had been planned out for me, at least, until God showed up. Now, I'm still a contractor, but I'm contracting people's destinies back to God. See? Everybody has a personal testimony.

Apostle Paul wrote, "He that calls you is faithful, and He will do it."[6] Every call from God enjoys divine support. There are certain things that you attempt to do that you can do on your own, but there some things that God is under obligation by His own word to show up to do on your behalf. You will not have to accomplish those things using your own strength or resources but with angelic help. When Jesus sent out His disciples in pairs, He gave them specific instructions not to take any money, extra shoes, or extra clothing. He told them that the laborer is worthy of his hirer.[7] In other words, He was saying, "Don't use your own resources. Use mine because they are granted and guaranteed only while you are on-mission in my name."

---

6 1st Thessalonians 5:24
7 Mark 6:8

The thing that is most important to God is the fulfillment of your assignment. There is a divine backup when you are on God's mission. God doesn't operate like human begins. He never disappoints. He is a faithful God, and He will do it. You have grace! I need you to say that till you believe it! God has given everyone a measure of grace.[8] I pray that this grace finds expression in your life.

Titus wrote, "The grace of God that brings salvation has appeared to all men."[9] To each one of us, grace was given according to the measure of Christ's gift. When Jesus ascended on high, He led capacity captive and gave gifts to men.[10] Take note of the word "gifts." He wasn't referring to money or stuff, nothing intangible. He was talking about people. These gifts are Apostles, some, Prophets, some, Evangelists, and some, Pastors and others, Teachers. You are a gift! You are a gift! You are a gift to your world. Never forget that.

When you find your area of calling in life, you find that niche where you add value to other people's lives. You are designed to be a blessing. You have a calling that is backed by grace. When you step into your call, you activate the grace reserved for you. When you are a giver, you are already blessed because it is more blessed to give than to receive.[11] When you give, it will be given back to you in good measure, pressed down, shaken together, and running over. [12] I need you to declare it again and again, "I am a gift to my generation."

---

8 Ephesians 4:7
9 Titus 2:11
10 Ephesians 4:7-8
11 Acts 20:35
12 Luke 6:38

The Gifts of Grace

Let's dig a little deeper into these gifts. For example, those called to be apostles. Do you know that God did not have church buildings in mind when He inspired the writing of this scripture? The truth is that God had the community in mind, not a building. We have diluted the power behind this calling due to our "church mindset." Apostles are pioneers. They are foundation layers. They are, in fact, like entrepreneurs; they take ideas and turn them into reality, creating a paradigm shift in entire communities, which makes life better for everyone else. They are pioneers. They are starters.

Prophets are dreamers. They are innovators. These are people who capture the future before other people have the opportunity to get there. You should know that interestingly, innovators are not essentially rich people. The person who conceives an idea may not have the capacity to make it a reality. That's where the gift of apostleship comes in. Apostles can take this new idea and make it happen. Dreamers can see. They see the finished project, just like an architect. The architect sees the building and creates a blueprint, but it is the builder that turns that dream into a reality.

Some gifts are Evangelists. I see these people as marketers and salespeople. They have the capacity to publicize and bring awareness. They can talk and explain processes and procedures. They can share the benefits and goals. Pastors can be seen as managers. They manage the details and keep things running. They manage human resources, teams, and help to provide care and counsel.

Teachers are like a trainer or consultant. People with a teaching grace are problem solvers. When they step in, God can bend natural laws to get problems solved. You need these types of gifts in your organization. They bring clarity in confusion and organization in chaos. They inspire, uplift, exhort, and bring growth.

There are other gifts. We have the gifts of healing. These people bring restoration because that is what healing is. We have 'helps.' Some people are designed to support and bring stability. It isn't everyone that is wired to pioneer a work. Do you know that it takes grace to assist a visionary? It takes grace. Some assistants rather choose to pioneer and end up having challenges. There are other gifts like administration, varieties of tongues, and more.

The scriptures say, "Having then gifts differing according to the grace that is given to us, let us use them: if prophecy, let us prophesy in proportion to our faith; or ministry or service, let us use it in our ministering."[13] When you come across the word "ministry," you may be thinking it refers to church work solely. Nothing could be further from the truth. Ministry simply means service. Whatever service you provide, according to the grace that has been given to you, so serve.

I pray that God will open your eyes to see the places and spaces He has graced you for. Apostle Paul asked Jesus when he was knocked down from his horse, "Lord, what will you have me do?"[14] Moses received the calling to build a tabernacle for God, but it was s who was graced to build it. He was filled with the spirit of wisdom for construction. Can you confidently say that what you are doing right now in your life is what God sent you and graced you for? For someone reading this book, it is your season of supernatural repositioning. Plant yourself in the center of God's calling, and grace will be activated for your assignment.

13 Roman 12 vs 6-8
14 Acts 9:6

6

Grace is in your Gift

"Pursue love and desire spiritual gifts."

The Christian life was designed to be lived by grace, not with our own ability. The provision of grace is God's divine endowment for His heritage. We are saved by grace, and we are graced for God's call on our lives. How can we then think that we can live our lives by our own strength if we started the journey by grace? Grace multiplies human effort. It is the multiplier effect that guarantees exponential growth. With grace, your little effort produces greater results. When you take out grace, what you're left with is disgrace. A wise believer learns to rely on God's divine ability to empower human ability.

As I mentioned, every believer has a calling and has been equipped with gifts. The gifts and calling of God are irrevocable.[1] That is amazing news! The calling has to do with your life's assignment. It has to do with God's purpose for your life. Everyone has a calling. There is a general calling into the body of Christ. And then, there is a specific calling to a unique place of assignment in God. When you discover the call of God, you will also discover the gifts that God uses to decorate your calling. Finding the call unlocks the gifts of God for your assignment.

Since everyone has a calling, this means that everyone is gifted in some area. The challenge is that so many are ignorant of this. Life is best lived using those gifts. Apostle Paul wrote, "Earnestly desire the best gift and yet I show you a more excellent way."[2] There is a place for desiring gifts. The scriptures say, "Pursue love and desire spiritual gifts."[3] I can tell you that I am through running my life on human ability. That's what happens when you have tasted what is called the anointing. I have tasted grace and discovered that it takes much more effort to fail than it takes to succeed when you walk in grace.

The Secret of Success

Look around any major city, and you will see people working hard every day, sweating and toiling to make ends meet, struggling to climb up the corporate ladders of their careers. If hard work were the key to success, they would have succeeded a long time ago. But I have seen people who do not exert themselves that much, and because of the grace of God over their lives, they get amazing results. I prefer to live my life that way. I want to live my life by grace. If you

---

1 Romans 11:29
2 1 Corinthians 12:31
3 1 Corinthians 14:1

also desire the same thing, the key is locating your gift, and focusing on your area of spiritual endowment.

Everyone has a gift. I encourage you to locate yours. There is no point in trying to be a photocopy of successful people. Some people try to box themselves into stereotypes that they have seen online or on TV. Everyone is trying to be like everyone else. Locate your gift! The body of Christ is beautiful in her diversity. We have diverse gifts, but in the end, everything works together. Find value in being yourself and staying true to who you are and who God has called you to be.

When I was coming up in ministry, I was serving under a very gifted man of God, Reverend George Adegboye. In fact, he was known around the world as a "mobile Bible" or "the walking concordance." He was always quoting scriptures off-hand without any effort. It was simply amazing how many scriptures he would produce back to back in a sermon. As I learned under him, my peers and I thought this was how ministry was to be done. If one of us preached a sermon, we would all be looking out for the number of scriptures quoted. We didn't realize this was a unique gift our pastor had.

Whenever a guest preacher came to speak, we would note how some would read one scripture only and spend the rest of the time expanding on that scripture and not quote another scripture. We began to measure the "Word depth" of preachers based on how many scriptures they could produce off-hand in their message. On average, you had to quote a hundred scriptures in a 60-minute sermon. By the time we were using scripture to explain another scripture, the whole premise would have been lost and confusing to the listeners.

Also, my pastor happened to be quite extroverted and bubbly. He preached with a lot of gesticulations and expressiveness. We all tried to preach like him. As far as we were concerned, this was the definition of success in ministry. The only thing was I felt quite uncomfortable preaching this way, as that wasn't my temperament. I wasn't one to gesticulate, shout, and jump around the stage as I preached. Each time I attempted to preach this way, I felt like a fake. I am so grateful that I came across a book titled "Transformed Temperaments" by Tim LaHaye. That was when I discovered that there are extroverts and introverts, and there was absolutely nothing wrong with being myself.

This was how God had made me, and it was perfect for my destiny. People that are extroverted, sociable, and very friendly are referred to as charismatic. After studying my personality, I discovered that I also had gifts. The word "gift" is also from the Greek word "Charis." So if you have gifts, you have charisma. There is power in simplicity. I don't need to copy any other person's personal style. My simplicity is a style on its own. I have nothing against those who have extroverted personalities, but when power is understated, it becomes even more powerful. Some of the people who make the loudest noise are the people who have nothing.

When I started out in ministry, I would receive invitations to different events with different interesting themes. Some of those event themes can give a preacher a headache. I remember the theme of an event was "The Unchanging Priesthood." Ok. The organizer apparently knew what they had in mind, but to the normal person, this was a difficult concept to understand. I love themes that are easy for people to relate. I do have a general teaching gift in the sense that I can teach on almost any topic, but I have an area of specialization – Success. The God kind of success and leadership.

Find your Niche, Find your Grace

God has taught me how to deliver myself from stress. Anytime I am given a topic, I always bring it back to my area of specialization. For example, if the topic is holiness, I will develop my teaching around "Holiness, the key to success." If the theme is marriage, I will speak about marital success. The principles are the same. Prayer? I'll make it, "Prayer – the Foundation for Success." Just like a soccer player will use their best foot, it's the same. Always play to the area of your strength. Not every opportunity is your opportunity, but when you find one that plays to your strengths, go for it. That is your opportunity.

It's time for you to begin placing value on the gifts that God has given to you. Never trivialize your gift, even if it is the gift of bringing humor and laughter. This is a gift. It's an industry on its own. People are building their careers around making others laugh and forget their issues even if it's for an hour. Who knows how many more industries there are left untapped? Find your niche. Find your gift. Find grace!

Don't allow anyone to put you into a box. Don't allow people to run your life based on their expectations of you. No one was there when God planned your life, nor were they there when He invested gifts into your life. So don't base your life on someone else's formula or journey. You can't put God in a box. God is the God of variety. He is original, and your path may just be completely different from the path people often think will lead to success.

Whatever God has called you to is exactly what you should give your focus to. There is a common misconception that being called into ministry requires having a church base. This is a big mistake. If God has not called you into church planting, don't do it because it will drag you down. Church growth isn't by human intelligence. It is by grace. You must learn to pray and learn firsthand from God how to fulfill your assignment. Ask God what to do per time.

New Grace, Old Mountains

In April 1994, I really felt stranded in life and ministry, and I began to pray. My wife and I decided to fast, and we went to Lekki beach to pray. When we got there, I began to pray, "Lord, I feel like things are not moving forward. What next?" And that day God spoke to me saying, "Keep on praying. Just continue to pray. I will tell you what to do. Keep praying." He then told me, "You have been flying over low mountains and hills before now, but now, I am bringing you to the place of higher mountains and hills. However, you are still flying at the old level. That is why you are colliding with the mountains. This is why you are experiencing obstacles." God said, "Come up higher. Continue this prayer and I will speak to you."

Not long after that, God spoke again, saying, "I am taking you to the next level through the gifts I have given you to teach scriptural success principles. You will do it on Radio, TV, seminars, tapes, publications." He continued, " You will not be able to do it in your present church, I am moving you out. You will start a church." And that was where God spoke to me about starting Daystar Christian Center. It was June of 1994. I can never forget.

So I moved. I discovered my gifts and realized it was God's

time to use it. I went on Radio and began to teach success principles, and it became my brand. I had not heard anyone do that in Nigeria before me. I thank God that I listened and obeyed. The rest is history. Listen, if you wake me up in the middle of the night and ask me about success, I can effortlessly speak about success for 24 hours nonstop. It is not a boast. It is the truth. As I read the scriptures, I keep seeing success principles on every page, from the first page of Genesis to the last page of Revelations. It's just natural for me. I am graced for it. I teach leadership, management, successful marriage, and more, all from the Bible. I am wired for it, born for it, graced for it.

I pray for you that you will discover every investment that God has put in your life. This comes by revelation. Apostle Paul said, "I did not receive it from man, nor was I taught it."[4] There are people that God is trying to use who keep running to people. God is trying to get your attention, but you are chasing after other men and women, looking for formulas and connections. Remember Samuel, when he was a boy, and God spoke to him? He ran to Eli, but Eli told him, "I am not the one who called you. I am not the one who spoke to you." This happened a second time until Eli recognized what was happening. God was speaking to the boy. We're always chasing after counsel. If you are not careful about who you're receiving counsel from, instead of being counseled, you can be canceled.

Who are you called to?

There is a remarkable story about what happened between the apostles Paul and Peter. Paul wrote; "But on the contrary, when they saw that the gospel for the uncircumcised has

---

4 Galatians 1:12

been committed to me as the gospel for the circumcised was to Peter; for he who worked effectively in Peter for the Apostleship to the circumcised also worked effectively in me towards the Gentiles." He said, " And when James, Cephas, and John, who seemed to be pillars, perceived the grace that had been given to me, they gave to me and Barnabas the right hand of fellowship that we should go to the Gentiles and they to the circumcised."[5] Wow! Isn't that interesting?

Up until that time, the gospel was only being preached to the Jews. But now, the disciples of Jesus began to see a peculiar grace upon Paul for ministry to the Gentiles. In fact, when Jesus Christ sent out His disciples to preach, He told them not to visit any homes of Samaritans or Gentiles. Their focus was to be on the Jews. All of a sudden, this man shows up with his own assignment to preach to the Gentiles. Can you imagine the drama this must have caused, especially with Paul's history? This would have been trending on social media in our day.

Can you understand why God kept Paul hidden from the church in the earlier part of his ministry? If he tried to use the methods and formula of his predecessors in ministry, he would have missed out on God's unique calling for his life. They now realized that this man, Apostle Paul, had a unique calling. They came to understand that the gospel for the uncircumcised had been committed to him, just as the gospel for the circumcised had been committed to Peter. The same way Peter was getting powerful results with the Jews was exactly how Paul was getting results with the Gentiles. It is interesting and remarkable, indeed.

---

5 Galatians 2:9

When Peter preached the good news to the Jews, there were results! When he tried to mix with the Gentiles, there was trouble. When Paul attempted to preach to the Jews, read it in the Bible, he ended up being beaten up. Wherever Paul went in the word to preach, the people who opposed and harassed him were Jews. It was like confusion followed him. They would beat him, slap him and even attempt to stone him. He would be insulted and spat on. But the same Paul, whenever he ministered to the Gentiles, great grace would release God's power. I hope this opens your eyes of understanding. Stop struggling. Find your place and space.

The Evidence of Grace

Grace is perceivable. If you have it, we will see it. Some people claim to have certain gifts, but you never see the evidence. Your gift should work. How can you claim to be a prophet and yet have no revelatory gifts? How can you claim to be called to sing, but the Holy Spirit takes a stroll when you start "singing" in a service? There is no harm in attempting to explore a particular gift, but as soon as you see that God's grace is not on it, you should drop it like a hot iron.

Grace is perceivable. It was when the disciples perceived that grace was upon Paul that they extended the right hand of fellowship. If you keep getting the "left foot of fellowship," maybe it's time to wake up. If there is no anointing on it, if there is no flow, there will be no provision for it. Healthy things grow. If you're not fulfilling your calling, you won't see the fruits of grace.

Use your Gift

You may ask: How do I develop my gifts? How do I get my gifts to work? There was a pastor who attended a service with a guest speaker at our church, and I remember him speaking to my wife. He told her that he remembered when she used to preach to herself alone in the classroom at school. Imagine preaching to an empty room, but look at the crowds we speak to today. Use your gift. Having then, gifts differing according to the grace that is given to us, let us use them.[6] Using them is the key. It's so sad when I see people that God has called into ministry who are waiting to use their gift only when they can speak to a large crowd. That isn't ministry. True ministry is meeting the needs of other people. I started out by teaching people one on one. I used to walk around with a small Bible in my back pocket. If I came across you and you had a few minutes to spare, rest assured, you would leave with some revelation. I started preaching in front of the mirror in my bathroom at home.

Joseph started out with interpreting his own dreams before getting to the palace, the big stage, to interpret Pharaoh's dreams. Start one on one. The gifts are not given to make you blow up; they are for meeting the needs in the lives of others. You prosper when you serve your world with your gifts. When you meet needs, you will become very valuable.

Are you still looking for opportunities? They are right in front of you. Use the one closest to you now. I started speaking in school fellowships, and then doors opened to preach in churches. With time, your gifts will mature and become refined. There is a law of use. It is a principle, and it works. When I first started teaching, I used to lash out at

___
6 Romans 12:6

people with my words. I thought I was being impressive, but by the time I was done speaking, I could see the confusion written clearly on the faces of my audience. Well, I have grown over the years. My gift is more refined.

Go out there and do what God is laying on your heart to do. There was a time I would preach, and all the honorarium I received was a bottle of Coca-Cola. On a lighter note, I remember a pastor that I preached for who came to see me. He had a brown envelope, and I got excited. I even requested a soft drink for him. As soon as he left, I opened the envelope, not wanting to be discourteous while he was around. What was inside? A letter of appreciation and a photo of me while I was speaking on stage! I didn't even like the photo. To be candid, the pastor was just starting out in ministry like me. They obviously did not have much in terms of financial resources too.

Develop your Gift

You know what I have discovered? If you put money first, then you will not make any progress. Focus instead on developing your gift. Develop it to the level of excellence. You increase the quality and quantity of what you offer, and what comes back to you will increase. Over the years, I have continued to develop and refine my gift. Now, when I speak for even a half-hour, I receive large amounts of money. My focus is not on the money, but on meeting needs with my gifts.

I pray for you that you will locate your calling, that you will receive revelation. God will do it. I pray that the God who spoke to me and called me, will speak to you. The One who helped me find my place will help you find yours. I declare that your gift will not go to waste.

7

Grace and Gratitude

"All that is within me bless His Holy Name."

Grace is a concept that evokes gratitude. It is unquantifiable. How do you measure something priceless, that has no financial comparison? The world's most expensive gems cannot compare to grace. There is absolutely nothing a human being will ever be able to do to pay for sin. You can't pay money to get rid of sin. Grace is a blessing that money can't buy. God gave us grace as a gift, as an act of benevolence. A gift, by definition, is free. This means there's absolutely no way you can pay for it. All the wealth combined on earth will not be enough to buy grace. It has been freely given.

By grace (or by gift) you have been saved through faith, and that (even that grace is) not of yourselves; it is the gift of God, not of works lest any man should boast.[1] When a person receives something they haven't worked for, it is a gift. As I mentioned earlier, the word grace is from the Greek word "Charis," which also means gift. God is so good! We receive forgiveness as a gift. So the question I have for you then is: How do you respond when you are offered a gift? You respond with gratitude.

Gratitude is the offering of thanks, a heart overflowing with praise and thanks for what you have received. Remember, you didn't work for it, so you should be thankful for it. Sin has plagued humanity from the beginning, but through the grace of God, we can receive redemption through the blood of Jesus. The expense, the guilt, the shame, the full payment became the burden Jesus carried on our behalf. Think about it. All we have to do is pray to God; He forgives us and wipes the slate clean. It sounds too good to be true, sometimes.

Our sin records are completely wiped clean. It's like you never committed the sin in the first place. We have become the righteousness of God in Christ Jesus.[2] Righteousness is a gift. The simplicity of it is the very reason it is so complicated for many Christians. We struggle with the thought of being sinless. When we ask for forgiveness, the heavens do not split with thunder and lightning. We don't see an angel hovering over us with a sword or rod. We don't see anything dramatic or spectacular, but the truth is we are still cleansed, but not by our power or might. It's so much easier to justify forgiveness by works, isn't it? Well, you simply cannot access what God has made provision for by grace through works.

1 Ephesians 2:8-9
2 Corinthians 5:21

It's almost like asking God to let you work for it. It's equivalent to telling God that forgiveness is too big for Him, and He needs your help. Once it seems like things aren't working in a particular area, we immediately switch into trying to help God. We start saying prayers such as, "Lord, you know how much I serve you. You know how hard I work in your church. You know how much I have prayed and fasted." But what God is saying is, "Exactly! That is the reason why this is not working, because it was not designed to run on the platform of what you have done. It has already been provided on the platform of what Jesus has done. Take it as a gift."

Receiving is an Art

You have got to be comfortable receiving things for free. Receive the free gift of salvation. Receiving God's blessings for free. No obligations and no caveats. There are no hidden fees. The fine print is all in your favor. And there should be an appropriate response to grace. There is a spirit of gratitude that keeps the stream of grace flowing. Grace is undeserved favor. Well, pride is not having a heart of gratitude, thinking you did it, or some of it in your power. It's equally bad when you think you deserve grace. It is undeserved. God has given grace in spite of us, in spite of our weaknesses.

If you have a good sense of value, you will not be comfortable remaining permanently on the receiving end. You will want to respond back in some way. Despite God giving us His grace for free, do you know how much He paid for it? Nothing is really free! Someone had to pay the price for you to receive this amazing gift of grace. Someone went through the fire so you would not have to. Before we knew Him, Christ died for us.[3]

---

3 Romans 5:8

I have had the opportunity to interact with people around the world, and I have come to realize that there are some people whose sense of value would not allow them to take something from you for free. Salvation may be free to you, but it is not free in value. Free does not mean zero value. Free means someone else paid for it. When you recognize the value of grace, you will respond in gratitude.

God has given me the wisdom to learn how to preserve the access He has given me to influential, powerful, wealthy, and highly resourced people. God told me, "Look, there are thousands of people making demands on them, sometimes hundreds of people." He said, "You need to position yourself in such a way that when someone hears that you are at their door, or sees your phone call, the person is not irritated; the person is not afraid to pick the call, and the person feels good about you. You need to separate yourself and the way to do that is not only to be a receiver, but to also be a giver."

An Attitude of Gratitude

When you position yourself as a giver as well as someone who knows how to receive, you are in the right place. So what do you give back to God? I believe that the proper response is gratitude. King David, the psalmist wrote, "Bless the Lord o my soul and all that is within me. Bless the Lord o my soul and do not forget."[4] I like David! He knew how to preach to himself. I love those psalms where he speaks directly to himself. "Why are you cast down O my soul. Hope in God." [5]You should talk to yourself like that sometimes. You may not be where you want to be, but remember that you are not where you have always been. What you look for is what you find.

---

4 Psalm 103:1-2
5 Psalm 42:5

Attitude is a choice. Having a heart of gratitude is the perfect response to life. It turns your focus away from what isn't working. Once your focus is on what isn't working, you will begin to discover more things that are not working. Rather, if you turn your focus to the things that are working, you will begin to take stock of the good things in your life, and you will soon see grace at work.

Oh, I have learned some hard lessons as a pastor. Can I confess my sins to you a little bit? In the early years of our church, we didn't have a lot of attendees, and I used to be really concerned about our Sunday attendance. I had developed a reputation with the ushers because they knew that I would be eagerly waiting for the headcount immediately after the service. You can believe that I would have done my own personal survey from my vantage point, so I validate the information the ushers would give me. Sometimes it would seem like there were more people in the service than the count the ushers would give me, and even worse, the count was sometimes less than the previous Sunday. Once the devil knew what my focus was, he knew what he could use to manipulate me.

My emotions and moods became connected to the numbers of attendees. I would get so frustrated because the numbers weren't increasing. At some point, out of frustration, I asked the ushers to stop counting. I had to find a way to stop getting myself worked up and frustrated every Sunday. I remember pulling our staff aside one day and taking them out on evangelism. I told them to go preach and invite people to church. In my calculations, even if all we received for our efforts was four to five people, that was good enough. And then, the next Sunday came, and we counted again. Attendance was even less than the previous Sunday.

I started to feel like I was getting to the point of shutting everything down.

But I was delivered. I told our ushers to stop counting, and I shifted my focus. For a few months, we didn't take any attendance. Now fast forward, sometime later, the church experienced a growth explosion. The Holy Spirit helped me develop some maturity. Why was I so focused on attendance? I had to stop looking at what wasn't working and focus on the things that were working. That is my question to you: What is your focus on?

Give Back Gratitude

Stop complaining and be a grateful person. Maya Angelo said, "If we give cheerfully and accept gratefully, everyone is blessed." This quote captures both ends of the spectrum. The giver should give cheerfully, and the receiver should receive gratefully. Even God loves a cheerful giver.[6] Even when I receive something I have paid for, I still respond with gratitude. People who have received grace should also have the capacity to give grace. Sometimes, we don't give because we think the recipients don't deserve it. But, see what Jesus says about that. He said, "You have heard, 'an eye for an eye, a tooth for a tooth. If somebody slaps you on the right, you return it'. He said, "no, don't do that. Bless those that curse you. Pray for those that despitefully use you and persecute you that you may be the children of your father. He causes the sun to rise both on the just and the unjust; both on those that deserve it and those that do not deserve it."[7] If you have received grace from God, you should have the capacity to extend grace to other people.

6 2 Corinthians 9:7
7 Matthew 5:38-48

There is a story about ten lepers in the Bible.[8] As Jesus was walking by, they saw Him and shouted, "Jesus have mercy on us." Jesus stopped, called them, and then told them to go show themselves to the priest. "Show yourselves to the priest," Jesus said, and they immediately obeyed. As they were going on the way, they suddenly discovered that they were healed, and one of them turned back. Instead of going to the priest, he turned back and headed back to Jesus – the provider of the free gift of healing. When he got to Jesus, with a loud voice, he glorified God.

Now, the fact that Jesus stopped what He was doing and called everybody's attention to what just happened is important. Jesus asked, "Were there not ten healed? Where are the nine? How come it is this Samaritan that has come back to give glory to God?" This means that what you do after God has blessed you is important to God.

There are often two groups. Those who respond with gratitude and those who take grace for granted. Our human nature gravitates towards the negative more than the positive, and I find this remarkable. We are apt to see the evil arrayed before us than the angel on our side. Your attitude is, however, your choice. It is now up to you. Stop looking for the devil, instead, look for God. Regardless of what the devil is up to, God is doing much more, exceedingly, abundantly more than you can imagine. What really matters is what God is up to.

Don't take Grace for Granted

The longer we have been Christians, the easier it is to take grace for granted. Don't you realize that even waking up

---

8 Luke 17:11-19

in the morning is by grace? Don't take the seemingly little things for granted. It isn't everyone who slept last night that made it through the night. Don't take it for granted when you have food to eat or clothes to wear. Never arrive at the point where you feel like you have worked for it, like you have earned it. If not for grace, we will be nothing.

When you leave your house and return in safety, give gratitude for God's grace. When you plan a project, and it becomes successful, now you know how to respond. Don't be like the nine who never came back. Be in the minority who come back rejoicing to God knowing fully well that the breakthrough is because of Him and Him only. God deserves your praise. Even when you need divine intervention, go on the frequency of gratitude.

You only need a few moments to think, and you will begin to realize how much grace is at work in your life. Oh, you will find something to thank Him for. Gratitude is the proper response to God's grace. Gratitude opens the heavens for the release of more grace. How about what could have happened that did not happen, and you know absolutely nothing about it? Give Him some praise, whether you can name it or not. You owe God some praise. He has been good to you. You went through hell and high waters, but the important thing is, you are still here. What happened to you would run someone else to the psyche ward, but you are still standing. Do you know that gratitude provokes the release of grace?

Engage life with gratitude, not with doubt, or anxiety. In my experience, I have come to understand how these things work. Human beings are like magnets. We have the power to attract or repel. Your attitude goes a long way when it comes to what you are believing for. For example, money and worry don't go hand in hand. The more you worry about money, the more it runs away from you. When Jesus was faced with a multitude who had not eaten for hours, He had a choice between worrying or being thankful. The only food they had access to was five loaves of bread and two fish. But Jesus did not complain or make a negative confession.

On the contrary, He gave thanks! And there was a multiplication of resources enough to feed the multitude and have leftovers. That is the power in having an attitude of gratitude.

When I was a teenager, I used to be so worried that I had furrows on my forehead. I worried about everything, the past, the present, and the future. I barely had any money in my pockets that it was so funny years after, in a hotel in the UK, I came across $1,000 in my pockets. I couldn't remember how it even got there, but I lifted it up to God and gave thanks. I was convinced that things had changed in my life because, previously, I couldn't even find a coin in all my clothing. Like my pastor says, when you see somebody with a long face, it shows that the person has a long way to go.

So when you are confronted with any situation, the first thing to do is ask God what He has to say about it. The revelation you receive from God will be the basis for thanksgiving. Once God has had a say about something, that's it! It's done. Your role then is to stand in the place of gratitude because it's already done. At this point, you're only waiting for the manifestation. Revelation from God changes your confession. You begin to confess on the frequency of faith rather than the frequency of fear.

Are you going to run your life based on the five senses? Switch to the spiritual dimension, the realm where God declares a thing, and it must come to pass. He honors His word more than His name.[9] Remember when Jesus visited the tomb of Lazarus. The man had been dead for four days, but Jesus declared that he was only sleeping. His prayer has some gems about gratitude. He said, "Father, I thank you that you hear me all the time, and I'm saying this, and I know that you always hear me, but because of the people who are standing by, I said this, that they may believe that you sent to me."[10] After saying this, Jesus cried out with a loud voice, and the dead man received life and came out. Jesus prayed out loud on purpose to teach us a principle. He gave thanks first!

I know that faith is rising once again in your heart as you read these words. Jesus confronted death with gratitude. Abraham was declared righteous before God because he did not doubt the promises of God and was empowered in faith as he gave praise and glory to God.[11] Complaining will not give you strength. It weakens and discourages. Take your eyes off of what is not working and look up to God with gratitude. Every negative situation will ultimately give in. Don't put a full stop where God has put a comma. And that's why I know that you are coming out of debt. You are coming into your wealthy place and recovering all you have lost in Jesus Name. Your days of borrowing and living month to month are over.

If Sarah could have a baby at 90, what are you facing that God cannot solve? Keep your focus on what God has said.

---

9 Psalm 138:2
10 John 11:41-44
11 Romans 4:20

He calls things that did not exist as though they did. Don't allow your circumstances to label you. Those who have laughed at you will soon see you laughing and rejoicing. Thanksgiving provokes the release of grace. You have been selected for divine intervention. You are on the list of God's overflowing abundance. You are a candidate for grace.

I pray for you that going forward, you will not take God's grace for granted. Are you reading this book and need grace for salvation? It's ever available. All you need to do is believe in Jesus. Ask for forgiveness of sins right now, because sin is man's greatest problem. Come to God with all honesty. He sees everything and gives grace abundantly. You are not reading this book by accident. God brought it to you this season to bring divine intervention into your life, destroy the power of sin, and release God's blessings into your life. The extent of your sin cannot compare with the manifold immeasurable grace that God gives. He first loved us and gave Himself as payment for our sins.

8

Grace for Solving Problems

"Who went about doing good."

There is absolutely no one in this world who will not face problems at one point or the other. The difference is in how we respond to the challenges and tests that come our way. How can we experience the miraculous or breakthroughs if there is nothing to break through? A real candidate for grace is someone who needs help. We need to stop being allergic to problems because they are simply the gateway for grace to become evident in our lives.

Uzziah, in the Bible, was marvelously helped until he became strong.[1] There are various degrees of divine help. In fact, you can get to that point in your walk with God that heaven comes to your aide in style.

Uzziah faced his challenges with so much divine help that at a point, they began to invent and innovate new military equipment and armory. His fighting strategy had changed, and he stopped fighting like everyone else. He wasn't alone. There was an invisible army fighting on his behalf. Some battles are way beyond human intelligence and capacity, and this is why you need to understand the grace you can access to demolish problems.

Grace is indeed for solving problems. Another way that I can describe God's grace is that it is divine help made available to you, which you did not deserve. This grace is released for specific challenges. Jesus said, "The Spirit of the Lord is upon me. He has anointed me…"[2] But Jesus didn't stop there. He went on to state what He was anointed for. "…to proclaim good news to the poor. He has sent me to proclaim freedom for the prisoners and recovery of sight for the blind, to set the oppressed free, to proclaim the year of the Lord's favor." What are you anointed for? Note that last line about the year of the Lord's favor or the acceptable year of the Lord. The acceptable year of the Lord in the Old Testament was the year of Jubilee. That was once every 50 years. One year, every 50 years was the year of Jubilee when all debts were forgiven. A whole nation would have the opportunity of starting afresh; there was not one single person who owed a dime after. Jesus said this is the reason why I have been anointed, I have been anointed to declare to everybody that

---

1 2 Chronicles 26
2 Luke 4:18-19

the Jubilee has come. And the exciting thing about Christ's declaration of the Jubilee was it now not going to be a cycle that took place once in 50 years anymore. It was going to be a jubilee forever.

Grace on Mission

The grace upon Jesus was for a mission. It had a purpose. That is why God could trust Jesus with power because it wasn't just about having power, it was about using power to fulfill God's will on the earth. It is written that, "… God anointed Jesus of Nazareth with the Holy Ghost and power. Who went about doing good, healing all that were oppressed of the devil."[3] When you read the gospels, you will see why He was so anointed. Jesus became a problem to problems. Oppression had to end. Demons had to flee. Sick people were restored back to health.

A lot of times, we do not receive the answers to our prayers because our own purposes for those requests do not align with God's own purpose. You ask, and you do not receive because you ask amiss.[4] There is a reason why and the answer is in the scriptures: "This is the confidence that we have in him, that if we ask according to His will, He hears us. And if we know that he hears us, then we know that we have the petition that we have requested from Him."[5] The first thing you want to do in prayer is to secure God's hearing. You have to talk about what He is interested in. This is a simple principle in communication. You can talk about anything you want to, but if you really want my attention, you need to talk about what is of interest to me.

---

3 Acts 10:38
4 James 4:3
5 John 5:14

So what are you anointed for? I am anointed to solve the problems of ignorance and poverty. Jesus was anointed for the sake of other people, not for Himself. He had no illness or sickness. He had never been broke; neither was He lacking anything. But He was indeed graced for mighty acts. Why? Definitely not for Himself but for the people, for you and I. Grace is for solving problems. If you're not going to make any impact, then you don't have a desire for the anointing.

The Potency of Grace

I keep hearing about Christians praying for power, especially those who have been baptized in the Holy Spirit. Well, there seems to be some confusion at work here. Jesus said, "You will receive power when the Holy Spirit has come on you."[6] I believe that means that once you have received the Holy Spirit, you are already loaded with power. The thing that is lacking is the manifestation or expression of power. Power must have tangible results when used.

The early church was infused with power. The Bible says, "They went forth and preached everywhere, the Lord working with them confirming his word with signs following."[7] They were problem solvers, and so power followed and manifested. The number one problem everyone needs to solve is the sin problem. Every Christian has a responsibility to help other people solve that problem. The reason why many of us have never seen the Holy Spirit work in power in our lives is that we have never tried to help anybody solve the sin problem.

You may be wondering where to start. And I say this: The best opportunity you need to fulfill your destiny is the one at hand at the moment, the closest one to you. And the closest

6 Acts 1:18
7 Mark 16:20

opportunity to you right now could be in your family. It could be right there at home. It could be the person sitting next to you as you read this book. Even as anointed and graced as Jesus was, the first message He preached was not to a crowd. He started with solving problems at home. Need proof?

Remember the wedding that Jesus attended when He began His earthly ministry? They had run out of wine, which was a big deal in that culture. The only reason Mary could ask Jesus to help was that He had not been a liability at home. His mother had detected and tasted of the grace upon His life already. She knew there was something special about Him. To be irresponsible at home and expect to do something extraordinary in public is a waste of time. You know what Jesus said? He said, "Your Father who sees you in secret will reward you openly."[8] Public success must be built on the foundation of private success.

Embrace the Path and the Process

There is so much to learn from Jesus' earthly ministry. Jesus didn't launch his ministry by organizing the biggest crusade in town. He went by the seashore preaching to people one by one. Any organizational consultant or growth strategist would have told him that wasn't the way to build a huge following. We see huge crowds at crusades on TV and think it just happened by chance. No, it starts in the one on one. It begins with individuals. Jesus called twelve people first and look at how huge the global church is today.

After college, I was part of the Nigeria Youth Service Corp (NYSC), an initiative in Nigeria where college graduates are sent to different parts of the country to "serve" the nation.

---

8 Matthew 6:4

It was designed to expose graduates to other parts of the country and offer them opportunities to work and gain relevant experience, and to build relationships with people from other parts of the country, fostering unity. I remember having a small Bible that I carried around in my back pocket. Interestingly, I was the president of the Christian Corper's Fellowship in the state where I served. When I showed up at any of the homes of our members, they knew exactly what to do. They would immediately run to their rooms to get their Bibles. It was time for me to share the Word.

But I would hoard some of my supposed deep revelations. I thought I had to reserve those for when I was speaking in front of a large crowd. I would share basic insights and truths, saving up the "really good ones." That was until I discovered that my "deep revelations" weren't new at all. Someone had received the same special revelations twenty years before. I saw them in books. That taught me a lesson. The little bit of grace on your life is big enough for someone's breakthrough. Stop holding back. Start solving the little problems in your corner. Just like David, the big stage will come, but your success will be determined by what you have done in your private place.

You know, the more that I share the revelations I receive, the more I receive from God's Word. From sharing with individuals, I progressed to speaking at birthday ceremonies. A friend still has a photo of me speaking at his birthday party. We were in a living room, and there weren't too many people but hasn't everything changed today? I didn't have a job at that time, but I was creating one for myself. Listen, you are only jobless if you cannot find a problem to solve for someone, and grace is supplied for solving problems.

Grace does not Discriminate

There is a truth that guarantees an unlimited supply of grace. It is found in a story about Samson in the book of Judges. It says, "So, Samson went down to Timnah with his father and mother and came to the vineyards of Timnah. Now to his surprise, a young lion came roaring against him. And the Spirit of the Lord came mightily upon him, and he tore the lion apart as one would have torn apart a young goat though he had nothing in his hand. But he did not tell his father or his mother what he had done."[9] Look at that! The Spirit of God came upon him when he was confronted with a lion. Well, thank God for that young lion. Some of us will never know the grace of God upon our lives until we are faced with something that is beyond our ability.

Joseph did not become a prime minister tasked with solving a national problem overnight. Do you know where he started? He started by interpreting his own personal dreams and also ran errands for his father. It didn't matter what station or situation of life Joseph was in, he remained focused. Even Potiphar, his master in Egypt, saw that the Lord was with him.[10] Grace was available to Joseph in the pit, as a slave, in prison, and finally as prime minister, next in command to Pharaoh himself.

No problem should be too small for you to solve. There is no challenge that is beneath you. I pray that God will open your eyes to the opportunities that you have been ignoring for long. Embrace the call of God upon you and begin fixing things for your family, your local community, your church, and your business. Start small; grow big. I pray that you will experience open heavens over your life, in Jesus Name.

9 Judges 14:5-6
10 Genesis 39:3

Jesus went about doing good. That's the secret. Everywhere you go, you should be doing good. Every problem you come across should receive its termination letter just because you showed up.

Stop running away from problems. Face them head-on. Remember that you are not alone. There is grace in abundance unleashed for your assignment. If you leave an expensive car in the parking lot and simply admire it every day, while walking long distances every day, sweating to work and back, it will remain where it is. That sounds crazy, but that is precisely what many Christians do. We talk about exploits; we talk about miracles; we sing and dance, but we don't activate the grace that has been released for our lives. If you're going to experience grace, my question for you is: Where is the problem you're solving?

It's time to step out of your comfort zone. When you begin to walk in grace, the gifts of the Holy Spirit begin to find expression in your life. You step into the realm of, "eyes have not seen, ears have not heard; neither has it entered into the hearts of man." That is the realm of creativity and innovation. The gifts of God in your life are activated. The anointing for creativity is released upon you. You begin to solve problems like never before. I hope that you will take up this challenge.

A leader is someone who adds value to the lives of others, who solves problems. It takes grace. Whenever you show up, you will see a difference. The world around you will see a difference. Grace for exploits has been activated in your life. Things can never remain the same anymore. There is a stirring in your spirit as you read these words. There is a flame inside of you that is blazing forth. Your status has changed. Goliaths fall when you step on the scene. The long-standing issues that have plagued your family line are meeting their demise right now because something has been awakened in you. Your promotion is here.

9

Grace for Financial Success

"Everything you need and plenty left over to share with others."

God has called and graced me to empower people to break free from poverty and enjoy true success. So it's apt that we take some time to understand the relationship between grace and financial success. As you know, this is an area that has become challenging for many Christians to understand. In recent times, I have seen some debate on this very question, and in fact, it has even become a controversial issue. The question is: Is God interested in material and financial provision for Christians?

Some people claim the church has been preaching about prosperity for decades, and yet, what can Christians show for it. Some nations have strung spiritual movements and amazing churches, yet those countries now have the highest number of people living in extreme poverty. I think that something is wrong somewhere. There are now those who are suggesting that if you want to be wealthy, the church is not the place to go. But let's dig a little deeper into the core of this issue.

When I read the Old Testament scriptures, I see God's people living in prosperity, and you can easily attribute this to their relationship with God. There was Abraham, Isaac, Jacob, Joseph, David, Solomon, and so many more. Now, when we switch to the New Testament, the gospels to be precise, during the time of Jesus, what do you notice? There is no record of Jesus making anyone stupendously wealthy, but we do see that He was concerned about people not going without the basics like food and health. In fact, some of Jesus' notable miracles had to do with the provision of food. He also healed a lot of people.

Grace and Wealth

After His resurrection and ascension, and the birth of the New Testament church, can we find a direct relationship between the church and material wealth? The answer is in the scriptures. It says, "And God will generously provide all you need. Then you will always have everything you need and plenty left over to share with others."[1] First off, you have a promise from God that all your needs will be met, whether big or small. The key phrase is, "all you need." Having all that you need and plenty left over to share with

---

1 2 Corinthians 9:8 NLT

others doesn't look like poverty to me. If you have leftovers or surplus, that doesn't look like being broke. It is clear as rain that God wants to meet our needs.

Here's what I need you to remember: God's provision for you has been made on the platform of grace. Here's another scripture. " For you know the grace of our Lord Jesus Christ, that though He was rich, yet for your sake, He became poor, so that you through his poverty might become rich."[2] The beautiful thing is that God, knowing that we could never qualify on our own, sent His own son to pay the price for sin on our behalf. This is important to note because poverty is one of the repercussions of Adam's sin. The price that Christ paid for sin was equally paid for the consequences of sin. There was no poverty in our world until sin came. There were no sicknesses and diseases until sin came. What Jesus did that took care of sin also took care of all those things that came with sin; for instance, sicknesses and diseases.[3]

So when did Jesus become poor for our sake? This happened on the cross. He had everything, yet for you and I, Jesus became poor. So, if Jesus took your place and your price, you should take His place. The scriptures say, "For He has made Him to be sin for us who knew no sin that we may become the righteousness of God through Him."[4] So, when you accept what Jesus did on your behalf, something amazing happens. He takes the poverty, and if He has done that, you can accept the blessing.

As a Christian, you can't accept or claim poverty because Jesus already paid for that. This might be a difficult concept for some people to understand. Many have rejected grace

---

2 2 Corinthians 8:9
3 1 Peter 2:22-24
4 2 Corinthians 5:21

because they don't understand how to get free things. When something is powerful, valuable and it is coming to us as free, we are suspicious of it. Doesn't it always seem like there's a catch when things are free? We are used to striving, fighting, and toiling for things. When you are accustomed to struggling and hustling, it can be difficult to develop the capacity to receive the best things in life for free.

It's worth repeating again and again that what God has provided for you on the platform of grace, you cannot get it on the platform of human struggle. The wealth that Christians have in the spirit is beyond measure, but how do you activate the grace for financial success? I'll use the story of Abraham as a case study. The scriptures say, "What then shall we say that Abraham, our father, has found according to the flesh. For if Abraham was justified by works, that is, by human efforts, he has something to boast about but not before God. For what does the scripture say? Abraham believed God, and it was accounted to him for righteousness."[5] Here's the phrase to note: If you work for it, it is no longer grace.

It's like being employed. You do your work, and you receive your paycheck. A paycheck or salary is not a gift because you worked for it. When you work, you are owed a payment, but with grace, you receive it without works. The spirit of God is saying to someone reading this book right now, in the area of your finances, your human struggle cannot get what God has provided through the death and resurrection of Jesus Christ. So the spirit of God is saying to you, "Stop struggling. Receive your prosperity as a gift. It is already finished on the cross." Remember that as a Christian, things happen for you on two levels: first, the spiritual, and then

---

5 Romans 4:1-4

the physical. Bear that in mind, it is the same with your finances. That is the order. So you need to get this spiritual structure in place - prospering by grace and then in the physical; it will work exactly that way.

Switch to the Grace Channel

Abraham and Sarah struggled for years to have a child. They got to a point where Sarah became so desperate that she had an "amazing" idea. She offered her hand servant to Abraham, thinking that she could use an ownership concept or formula to help God. Just picture Abraham thinking that she had received this idea by divine revelation. I can even picture him thanking God for such an amazing and smart wife. But no, this was an act of desperation. Can you imagine offering your spouse to someone else? But you know what God did? He waited till Abraham and Sarah were completely beyond their natural ability to produce children, and then He made it happen. They had to get to the point where they let go, and they let God.

So you activate grace by faith. When you exercise total trust in God; you believe that you are who God says you are; you believe that what God has said is the reality in spite of contrary circumstances, that is, faith. It is that faith that activates grace. Stop struggling and let God's grace go to work on your behalf. You will love the results. It's time to switch from the works channel to the grace channel. The grace channel is so much better.

When you're an Abraham functioning with grace, you go down to Egypt and come out with silver and gold. When you are an Isaac, and there is strife over the wells you have dug, they realize that no matter how many times they challenge you, you keep pushing forward and digging new ones; they later come back to make a deal with you. You can't be stopped. God will set a table for you in the presence of your enemies and anoint your head with oil.[6] Listen, when grace is activated, there is no system built by man that can stop you from prospering because what you are receiving in the physical has already been provided in the spirit. Nothing can stop it.

So it is faith that activates grace. So how do you exercise faith in this area of finances? You believe that you are rich already. Your belief that you are rich is not based on what is in your bank account. It is based on what Jesus did on the cross. He became poor, and you became rich. It is irreversible. Except if the devil can carry Jesus back to the cross and 'unkill' him (permit my grammatical innovation). What Jesus did for us is irreversible. You became rich, so you are rich. So you say, "I am rich." Take your focus away from the current situation and look up to God from where your help comes.

I know that some will say that this is all about positive confession. No. It is more than that. There has to be an internal shift in how you understand grace, faith, and finances. In fact, if you attend a financial seminar anywhere that is not faith-based, the first thing they will tell you is that the major difference between a poor person and a rich person is not in their bank account, it is in their mindset. A rich person believes that he or she is rich. The rich believe that abundance is for them. That is it. I wrote it in my book, The Parable of Dollars, that the journey from rags to riches is, first of all, an internal trip. The place where a poor person first becomes rich is in the heart.

Stop using labels like you're one of the masses. Stop absorbing

---

6 Psalm 23:5

popular narratives about being part of the "common folk." 'Common' means cheap or readily available. You are anything but common. You are a peculiar person, rare, valuable, and unique. You are a peculiar person, a royal priesthood, and a holy generation.[7] Therefore if any man be in Christ he is a new creation; a new species.[8] No one has seen anyone like you before. You are one in your generation. You are in a class all by yourself.

The normal thing is to assume that the wealthy are stealing money or that some just got lucky. Once you think like that, you're programming yourself against grace. You're telling yourself to accept a system where only thieves have access to beautiful things. Don't mentally take yourself out of the class of people who enjoy the good things of life. I have had to fight mental battles for years, battling against insecurities when I was jobless, or when things weren't working out. But God gave me revelation, and I immediately began to attack my faulty mindset by saying, "I can never be poor again the rest of my life." I began to declare, "I am not a local champion, I am a world champion. I am going all over the world." At that time, it sounded ridiculous based on my physical conditions, but my identity in Christ remains constant. I am rich. I am prosperous. I am wealthy.

No Coincidences in Grace

My story is that of grace, pure grace. There is no other way to explain it. As a minister of the gospel, the value I provide is not by selling but by giving freely. However, the principle remains true that if value goes from you, value must come back to you. My "business" is to ensure that God's power, wisdom, and grace are flowing through me to solve problems

---

7 1 Peter 2:9
8 2 Corinthians 5:17

for people, thereby adding value to their lives. God takes care of how the value comes back.

My family and I went on vacation many years ago to EuroDisney in Paris. We arrived at the park in the morning with the kids, and then I realized we needed cash for the rides. I turned to my wife, Nike, saying, "I wished we had gone to use an ATM in the city before we came here." As I was saying that, out of nowhere, a family that was passing by stopped and greeted us. I was surprised they knew my name, as I couldn't recognize them. They told me that my brother had come to preach at their church. In fact, they had never met me in person. The next moment, he reached into his bag and pulled out some crisp Euro currency and gave them to me. They left, saying, "God bless you, Sir. Enjoy your ride." As they walked away, I just broke into a smile, saying, "Father God, even here in Paris, you did not allow me to get through saying what our need was, you had organized this blessing. This is sweet."

You might say that this was just coincidence, and I'll have no argument with you, but when coincidence becomes consistent, that's no longer coincidence; it is grace. This might shock you. A few years after the incident at EuroDisney, I took a flight from Lagos to Calabar in Nigeria. On the flight, I noticed a lady who read her Bible throughout the flight. I was quite impressed by her focus. When we arrived, we greeted each other in passing, but she walked up to me. She said, "I know you may not remember me. Let me show you something." She then opened the Bible and showed me a picture. I immediately recognized her! It was the same family that had blessed us at EuroDisney. I said, "Oh my God, I have been talking about you everywhere since then. God bless you." She responded with an amen, took out an envelope from that Bible, and handed the envelope to me. When I got in my car, I opened the envelope and saw half a million Naira. Another coincidence?

That's the interesting thing. I have countless stories that I can share similar occurrences. Don't blame me. It's not my fault, it is just grace. Stop struggling. I had been through it. You will go through the season of testing, and you will have the opportunity to choose whether you are going to trust God or whether you are going to believe what God has said. Even when your situation seems to be driving you crazy, God will help you if you have made a choice to do it by grace. The Spirit of God will help you to hold on. Hold on even when it is tight and difficult. God will always show up on your behalf in amazing ways.

I am sure you know the principle of exchange of value works differently in the for-profit space. I operate there too, so I know. You actually put a price on your goods and services, and people pay for them. Grace works in that space too. It makes you creative, and people pay for your services. Grace made Joseph provide solutions to national problems. He was promoted. David played the harp under the anointing and was invited to the palace to solve problems for the king. Grace will put the extra on your ordinary in your career.

The Mindset of Rest

The key factor is that the provision that God has made for the Christian is not made on the platform of works; it is made on the platform of God's grace. It is actually a gift. You access it through God's help, through God's power. Once you step out of the frequency of grace, you will not be able to access your provision, God's way. Remember that it is by believing what Christ did for us and accepting what God has done as our reality. This is what activates grace.

For a Christian, this is the way it works. Your provision is created in the spiritual; your breakthrough, your freedom, whatever it is, God is giving you is created first as a reality in the realm of the spirit, and then it translates into the physical realm for you. In the Bible, Christ is described as the lamb that was slain from the foundation of the world.[9] So that work that Jesus did on the cross was actually finished spiritually from the foundation of the world. So whatever it produces in your life was also finished from the foundation of the world. You have stepped into the realm of rest. Don't do anything from the platform of anxiety. It is not a matter of chance or luck. It is inevitable. So there is a rest for the people of God.

The Bible says, "..for anyone who has entered God's rest also rests from his own works, just as God did from His."[10] Wow! I love this. If God has already done it and is resting, why are you struggling? Allow God to do it, and all you have to do is accept the finished work. Jesus confirmed this principle when He said, "The Son can do nothing by himself, but whatever he sees the Father doing. For whatever the Father does, the Son does in like manner."[11] Jesus was saying that He was only doing what God had already done. His prayer time must have been really exciting. He would have seen those miracles happen in the spiritual dimension before they manifested in the physical realm.

The Place of Works

There is a clear disconnect in the relationship between works and grace. Sometimes, we think grace means we sit down,

9 Revelations 13:8
10 Hebrews 4:10
11 John 5:19-20

become lazy, and do nothing. Grace is an active agent, but it needs you to do something for it to be activated. You need to take action in the physical world for your spiritual reality to produce for you. Grace won't work if you don't work. Remember Abraham and Sarah? What if they had not consummated after God had released grace upon them? Can you imagine that? You have a responsibility to respond.

Let me clear things up for you. No amount of works can produce grace in our lives, but no matter how graced you are, if you don't work, what will the grace do? It will remain an inactive agent. Anything that is multiplied by zero, no matter how huge that number is, will always result in zero. The more grace you have on your life, the more you should be putting it to work. Paul the Apostle said, "But by the grace of God I am what I am, and his grace toward me was not in vain. On the contrary, I worked harder than any of them, though it was not I, but the grace of God that is with me."[12] The works come in after you have received grace. Grace can be wasted.

Grace amplifies your capacity to add value to people's lives by solving their problems. Accept the responsibility to work (produce value), and grace will be activated as you trust in the power of God, which is released to help you. This is how you produce extraordinary results. Grace will supply what you will sell to your world. You have the responsibility to package it, to present it; to position it for your world, and to give it out in exchange for value. Wake up! You already have grace. It is available in abundance.

Jesus called twelve, who became His disciples. He then gave power over unclean spirits, and the power to heal different types of sicknesses and diseases. Afterward, He sent them

---

12 1 Corinthians 15:10

out in pairs to go put the grace on their lives to work. He said, "Do not take any extra money. The laborer is worthy of his wages."[13] In other words, Jesus was saying that this principle never fails. If value goes out from you, value will come back to you.

Grace and Giving

There is another important principle of adding value, and it is giving. It is something that has become a very controversial topic. The Bible says, "Remember this—a farmer who plants only a few seeds will get a small crop. But the one who plants generously will get a generous crop. You must each decide in your heart how much to give. And don't give reluctantly or in response to pressure. "For God loves a person who gives cheerfully." And God will generously provide all you need. Then you will always have everything you need and plenty left over to share with others."[14]

God will generously provide all you need, so you will always have everything you need and plenty left over to share with others. Remember that God is the one who provides seed for the farmer and then bread to eat. In the same way, He will provide and increase your resources and then produce a great harvest of generosity for you. There is a mindset of abundance and faith in the grace of God that take will you from the realm of hoarding to the realm of overflow. Stealing or cheating is a sure sign of a lack of faith in the grace of God. In fact, it is written, "Let him that stole, steal no longer. But rather let him work with his hands what is good that he may have to give."[15]

Stealing is a terrible strategy for living a prosperous life. It's

13 Luke 10:7
14 2 Corinthians 9:6-8
15 Ephesians 4:28

always a matter of time before it all comes crashing down. Do not develop the mindset that likes to get value for

nothing. It's just like begging when you take something from someone without adding value in exchange. There is no grace on begging. Begging does not diminish the giver; it diminishes the receiver. We often carry this faulty perspective into the Christian faith. That is why we ask, and we do not receive because we ask wrongly to consume it on our selfish desires.[16] Begging or stealing isn't part of the values of the Kingdom of God.

Your giving has to align with your mindset. Think about it. When do you give reluctantly? This happens when you're not expecting much value in return. You need to start giving with revelation, not giving from pressure. It is the revelation that you have received that causes you to rejoice as you give, willingly and cheerfully, not out of compulsion. Paul the Apostle says, "And God will generously provide all you need. Then you will always have everything you need and plenty left over to share with others."[17] You see the way it works? It is like a cycle. You receive by grace, then you give. Freely have you received, freely give.

One person gives freely yet gains even more. Another withholds unduly but comes to poverty. [18] Is that not amazing? A generous person will prosper, and whoever refreshes others will be refreshed. That's because grace is always flowing, and if you position yourself rightly, it will continue to flow through you. You become motivated by God's love, and you become a conduit of grace. And that is why it is essential to place emphasis on helping the poor.

16 James 4:3
17 2 Corinthians 9:8
18 Proverbs 11:24-25 NIV

Whoever gives to the poor is lending to the Lord. Wow! That should change your mindset. Some of the core needs of the poor are food, clothing, and shelter. We should be fully engaged in our families and churches by providing for the needy. It was the same pattern in the time of the apostles. This was what they did with their money. There was a strong emphasis on caring for the needy. They were so focused on this mission that some sold their lands and expensive items and brought them to the apostles.

Great generosity is always borne out of great grace. The scriptures say," All the believers were one in heart and mind. No one claimed that any of their possessions was their own, but they shared everything they had. With great power, the apostles continued to testify to the resurrection of the Lord Jesus. And God's grace was so powerfully at work in them all that there were no needy persons among them. For from time to time those who owned land or houses sold them, brought the money from the sales and put it at the apostles' feet, and it was distributed to anyone who had need."[19]

Many years ago, the Holy Spirit woke me from sleep and said, "Your Mercedes car give it." That was my second car. The first one was sold by instruction from the Holy Spirit, and the money was given to the church. The second one, the instruction was clear to give it away that same day. I obeyed immediately! I have come to understand that obedience is the key. I didn't know why the Holy Spirit insisted I should send the gift that day, but I learned later that it was the wedding anniversary of the recipient. Well, I've been blessed several times over. God has provided for us spiritually, but it is our obedience to the Holy Spirit that allows God's grace to have a practical effect on our finances. This revelation of grace has changed my life completely. I pray that it will change yours too.

---

19 Acts 4:32-40

A PRAYER FOR YOU

I pray for the person reading this book who says, "Please pray with me that God should forgive me all my sins. My relationship with God is not okay." Or you may be asking God for a fresh release of grace for your life. Can you please put your hand on your heart? I want you to read this prayer out loud if you can.

Dear God, I believe that Jesus paid for my sins. I ask you to forgive me and to accept me as your child. Thank you for hearing my prayer, in Jesus name.

Let me pray for you:

Heavenly Father, thank you for the person who read this book. I thank you, Heavenly Father, because I know that their sins are forgiven, and the nature of sin is removed from them. Thank you, Lord. Heavenly Father, teach them to know you personally and teach them to love you and to love other people the rest of their lives, in Jesus name.

I prophesy in the name of Jesus Christ that the days of feeling powerless are over. Receive a fresh outpouring of God's grace through the Holy Spirit in Jesus' name. Receive a new sense of identity as a child of God, a victor, and a solution provider. The days of holding back are over forever. The days of holding onto little are over forever. In the mighty name of Jesus, I prophesy grace for generosity. And I prophesy that as grace flows from you to others, God's grace will be poured out even more on you. The days of delay and struggling over finances are over forever. I prophesy the days of miracles; the days of promotion; the days of restoration are here in the name of Jesus Christ! Thank you, Lord.

FOR OTHER TITLES
BY THE AUTHOR

Visit:

www.samadeyemi.net

www.successpower.tv

ABOUT THE AUTHOR

Sam Adeyemi, an insightful teacher, pastor and strategic leadership expert, co-founded Daystar Christian Centre, a multi-faceted church with tens of thousands attending services weekly and based in Lagos, Nigeria, with his wife, Nike, in 1995. The church is known for its vision to raise role models in the society and for its practical teachings and community impact programs. He is also the founder of the Daystar Leadership Academy, Success Power International and Sam Adeyemi GLC Inc. He and Nike are blessed with three amazing children, and they both mentor leaders and speak at conferences globally.

* 9 7 8 1 9 4 3 4 8 5 0 7 9 *